Avoiding Medical Malpractice

A Physician's Guide to the Law

W0230173

Avoiding Medical Malpractice

A Physician's Guide to the Law

William T. Choctaw, MD, JD

 Springer

William T. Choctaw, MD, JD
Chief of Surgery, Citrus Valley Medical Center
Clinical Faculty, University of Southern California
Keck School of Medicine
Los Angeles, CA, USA

ISBN: 978-0-387-73063-9   e-ISBN: 978-0-387-73064-6

Library of Congress Control Number: 2008922188

Printed on acid-free paper

9 8 7 6 5 4 3 2 1

springer.com

TO

Lorena
Priest, Preston, Dwight, Esteban, Amanda, Isabel, Aaliyah,
and
Vincent Julius Choctaw

Acknowledgments

I am grateful to the surgical care associates' physicians who have graciously shared their personal experiences regarding medical legal issues with me over the years. I am humbled and grateful to the entire 600-member physician medical staff at Citrus Valley Medical Center for electing me Chief of Staff, Chief of Surgery, and allowing me to serve for 10 consecutive years as a member of the Medical Executive Committee. I am thankful for lecture opportunities given to me by medical staff directors and hospital Continuing Medical Education (CME) directors throughout the country. They have extended me the privilege to speak to their hospital and medical staff leaders on many topics in this book. I am thankful to Lila SanNicolas who strongly encouraged me to give lectures, and to Dr. Ira Kodner, who introduced me to the Springer Publishing Company.

I especially appreciate the assistance of Dr. Esteban Ramirez, a second-year resident at Genesys Regional Medical Center. He was able to give me the new physician's perspective on many issues addressed in this text. I am very grateful to Irene Bourdon for her advice, support, and the technical assistance provided by her team, Steve Miller and Gale Scalzi.

I am also extremely grateful to my editors, Paula Callaghan, Lindsey Reilly, Susan Kreml, and Sethumadavan Prasad of the Springer Publishing Company. They have been tireless in their efforts to provide assistance for this literary project. I am forever humbled by the opportunity to be able to put my thoughts, beliefs, and concerns in writing.

Finally, I especially acknowledge my wife and best friend Lorena, without whose love, encouragement, assistance, and patience this project would have never been completed. She is and continues to be my guardian angel.

Contents

Introduction

Medical malpractice is a major challenge for the 21st century physician. It is associated with other comorbid legal problems doctors must face. The association between medical malpractice and disruptive physician behavior may at first glance seem remote. Malpractice has an evidentiary genesis that requires the satisfaction of very specific elements [1]. Disruptive behavior is a vague term that is poorly defined. Nevertheless, each has a significant impact on the doctor's ability to practice medicine. Their impact can cause considerable consequences over time.

Medical malpractice lawsuits are much more common now than they were when I graduated from Yale University School of Medicine in the early 1970s. This litigation has now contributed to a malpractice insurance crisis in our country. Many physicians can no longer afford medical malpractice insurance, or refuse to buy it, or have retired from the practice of medicine altogether because of it [2]. In my last 25 years of surgical practice, including the past 10 years as a lecturer and medical–legal consultant, I have seen a significant increase in the merger of law and medicine. This legalization of medicine has caused increased anger and frustration among physicians, leading to a decline in the quality environment of medical practice and, sometimes, to a decline in quality patient care and patient safety. The anxiety of this legalization has created an environment that can lead to disruptive behavior among the medical team members. It also contributes to a disproportionate number of physicians leaving the practice of medicine, decreasing the number of doctors available to care for patients. This crisis has forced many doctors to practice defensive medicine, further exacerbating the rising cost of healthcare.

I believe I am in a unique position to inform and help educate physicians about the law because I am a practicing physician with a law degree. Books on medical malpractice frequently are written by attorney authors for doctors to read. Other malpractice texts are written by those who have never actually practiced medicine on a daily basis in private medical practice. Arguably, malpractice is more acute for those physicians in private practice. In my surgical practice, I treat patients daily and must navigate the same treacherous medical–legal waters as other clinical providers. In addition, I have given many medical–legal lectures to hospital medical staffs, medical conferences, and medical students in the past 15 years [3]. Recently, the University of Southern California Keck School of Medicine invited me to give a series of lectures to their surgical interns and residents on medical–legal issues. Years ago it would have been unimaginable for surgical interns and residents to hear lectures about malpractice issues. Today, it is a new reality. Medical schools now understand the new medical–legal paradigm in medical education for future physicians. Now, it is rare to read a medical journal and not find an article on a medical–legal issue.

The national healthcare crisis in our country is primarily a malpractice tort reform crisis for physicians [4]. Now is the time for all physicians to be educated about the Rule of Law and various regulatory agencies that impact our ability to care for patients. The Joint Commission for Healthcare Organizations has made patient safety its top priority. Patient safety is a euphemism for "avoiding medical mistakes." The Institute of Medicine recently reported that 48,000 to 98,000 patients die annually because of medical mistakes made by doctors and hospitals [5]. Federal and State legislatures are requiring unprecedented reporting of morbidity and mortality data on a hospital- and physician-specific basis [6]. Increased Internet access makes it easier for the public to view this information. All these factors contribute to a potentially more perilous medical–legal environment for physicians. Nevertheless, the practice of medicine continues to provide many new and exciting opportunities along with challenges. Some of these challenges are in the areas of cybermedicine and telemedicine. Also, the science of litigation is a new approach to combat medical malpractice that is presently in its infancy.

Finally, I have been privileged to serve two elected terms as Mayor of the City of Walnut, California (while still practicing medicine full time). I understand the public's concerns and how public fears of healthcare may influence medical–legal circumstances. Doctors in academic and private practice and residents, interns, and medical students all face unique issues that I attempt to address in this volume. I have seen these issues in both academic and private practice.

However, regardless of all the issues we face in practicing medicine today, it is important for us doctors to remember that life is but a journey that we should embrace and enjoy!

1

Basic Law 101: The Journey Begins

Knowledge is Power.
Francis Bacon

In the United States of America, we are fortunate to live in the world's greatest democracy. Our Constitution is the progeny of the Magna Carta ratified by the English Parliament in 1215 [7]. The Rule of Law as defined in our Constitution governs our democracy [7,8]. Our government has three branches: the executive branch enforces the law, the judicial branch interprets the law, and the legislative branch creates the law. Our legal system can be further divided administratively into **federal** and **state** levels. These two levels are the primary sources of law in our country.

Federal law is created in Washington, D.C., signed by the President of the United States, and applies to all 50 states equally. State law is created in the individual state's capital, signed by the state's governor, and applies to that individual state only. State laws regarding the same issue may differ from state to state in both tone and application. Medical malpractice is a state law [4,9]. However, federal laws may establish national guidelines that mitigate or further modify the application of state medical malpractice.

An attempt at the federal level to influence malpractice litigation was made recently when Congress tried unsuccessfully to pass a tort reform package that would place a $250,000 cap on damages awarded for pain and suffering. The reform package died in the United States Senate [10]. The federal government may also extensively influence physician liability beyond medical malpractice. An example of this influence is the National Practitioner Data Bank (NPDB) [11].

The NPDB is an electronic bank of all payments made for physicians (practitioners) in association with medical malpractice settlements or judgments as well as adverse peer review actions taken against the physician. By federal law, all medical malpractice payments and certain adverse actions including disruptive behavior must be reported to the NPDB. In response, the NPDB is required to make this information available to hospitals, state license boards, some professional societies, and other health entities under certain circumstances [12]. The five areas that are reported to the NPDB are as follows:

1. Professional liability payments made on behalf of a physician.
2. Adverse action reports based on the physician's professional competence or misconduct (aberrant behavior) that result in reduction, restriction, suspension, revocation, denial, or nonrenewal of the physician's privileges for more than 30 days. It also includes the doctor's voluntary surrender or restriction of privileges either while under investigation or in place of an investigation.
3. Disciplinary actions associated with professional competence or misconduct taken against a practitioner's license including revocation, suspension, censure, reprimand, probation, and license surrender.
4. Professional society actions taken for reasons of competence or conduct that adversely affect membership in the professional society.
5. Medicare and Medicaid exclusion reports containing action against a physician causing exclusion from these programs because of fraud and abuse.

If the foregoing five areas look familiar, it is because they are a part of every single credentialing application we fill out for appointment and reappointment to hospital medical staffs, HMOs (health management organizations), etc. The stated purpose of the NPDB is to prevent problem physicians, when they get into difficulty, from moving to a different location without having their issues of competence and conduct adequately addressed. All information in the data bank is supposed to be confidential. In reality, reporting the number and amount of claims settled is not an accurate indication of how professionally competent a physician is in practice (think nuisance suits). Additionally, the information in the National Practitioner Data Bank is not always either accurate or kept confidential. It is important for all physicians to periodically review online their personal NPDB information to assure its accuracy. Thus, as providers we must keep in mind, when in settlement meetings for malpractice claims, that the agreed-upon proceedings and amounts will be released to hospitals and possibly to the general public [13].

There are two main court systems in this country: federal courts and state courts. Because medical malpractice is under state law, malpractice litigation is initially heard in a state court. State court systems are divided into three levels: the court of general jurisdiction, the intermediate appellate courts, and the court of last resort. Malpractice litigation is usually heard in the court of general jurisdiction in most states. There are two main types of law categories: **civil law** and **criminal law** [14]. If you are found guilty of violating civil law you are considered liable to the individual plaintiff and you pay money damages for injury to said plaintiff. If, on the other hand, you are found guilty of violating a criminal law, you are considered to have injured society as a whole and you may go to jail in addition to possibly paying money damages. Medical malpractice is exemplary of a civil law violation. Thus, the violator pays money damages to the patient plaintiff for injuries caused by the physician's alleged negligent act. The most expensive malpractice allegations include errors in diagnosis and medication errors.

MOST EXPENSIVE ALLEGATIONS
- Improper performance
- Errors in diagnosis
- Failure to supervise or monitor
- Medication errors

A number of diseases are associated with errors in diagnosis, including breast cancer and acute appendicitis. Rarely are criminal charges associated with malpractice proceedings.

COMMON ERRORS IN DIAGNOSIS
■ Breast cancer
■ Cancer of lung/bronchus
■ Appendicitis
■ Colorectal cancer

Nevertheless, above the traditional tort law of negligence is a category called criminal negligence [15]. For example, if I drive my car at 100 miles an hour on a desolate interstate highway and I injure someone walking, I am negligent. I would have theoretically acted in a way that is below the standard of how one would expect a reasonable and prudent person driving a car to act. If on the other hand, I drive my car 100 miles per hour within the city on a crowded downtown street with pedestrians and I injure someone, I would have acted recklessly. By acting recklessly, my actions are so egregious and below what a reasonable prudent person driving a car would do that the court can imply intent on my part. In other words, I should have known it would be highly likely that my actions would injure someone whether I purposely tried to hit someone with my car or not. If the facts and circumstances allow opposing counsel to prove implied intent, I can be charged with criminal negligence. In the medical context, a physician would probably need to be incapacitated somehow, before making some horrible medical mistake, to be found criminally negligent. It would require a medical action under very extreme and unusual circumstances. Nevertheless, legal interpretations are constantly changing. Fortunately, allegations of criminal negligence against physicians are uncommon.

2
Shades of Gray

There is no black and white.

Having attended both medical school and law school, I have finally understood the difference between doctors and lawyers. The difference is in the way we think. In medical school, we are taught the scientific method of reasoning based on Koch's postulates [16]. It is a process that is logical and verifiable by the physical evidence we observe. For example, either my patient has acute appendicitis or he does not have acute appendicitis, based on the pathology report [17]. Medicine is primarily concerned with the result, less with the process. Medicine is black and white.

In law school, we are taught that there is no black and white; there are only shades of gray. The law is primarily concerned with the analysis of the process, less with the result. A legal conclusion is based on an analysis, which is based on how the facts are applied to the existing law or rule. Every law or rule has an exception or qualification. Indeed, much of our time in law school was devoted to learning about the exceptions to the law! This grayness concept in the law is very uncomfortable and frustrating for most doctors, especially surgeons. As surgeons, we like exactness, clarity, and structure.

Additionally, the law may be expressed (written) or implied (between the lines). This implied quality of the law adds a layer of abstractness that increases the complexity of the law. Indeed, it is this abstractness that makes the law deceptively complex. For example, the concept "use a gun, go to prison" seems very clear and straightforward. Nevertheless, whether the one who uses a gun will actually go to prison always depends (grayness) on the circumstances. This abstractness flows to the person such that the results may vary with each individual perspective and set of facts involved. It may not only vary with the individual perspective but have a chameleon-like quality, causing it to change with each environment or set of circumstances. Implied law also occurs in the legal phrases and legal terms of art. A member of the public or a doctor may have an intellectual understanding of the term "informed consent," but legally it has a very specific meaning. The public generally views the phrase "assault and battery" as to hit or batter someone. However, the law defines assault and battery as merely unpermitted touching or the fear of unpermitted touching [14]. Legally, it is a more subtle and broader definition. The implied law is very powerful for the patient plaintiff or government agency but most frightening for an individual physician defendant. Therefore, the physician caregiver is not in a very comfortable environment when any litigation develops.

Grayness invokes a counterintuitive reaction, especially from doctors. As scientists, we physicians live in a world of structure supported by verifiability. However, scientists constitute a minority influence in present-day society. Grayness is not verifiable because it changes constantly with each set of facts and circumstances. It is important for us to understand this concept of shades of gray because it is how much of the world operates, especially the legal world. Many bylaws, rules, and policies have interpretations as variable as the number of persons reviewing the document [18]. Moreover, the ultimate challenge comes from the need to develop a consensus on the exact meaning of any rule or policy.

3
The Triangle: Law–Medicine–Politics

Rapidly open surgery is becoming politically incorrect.
  David V. Cossman, MD.

In the 1980s, when I began private practice, the law had less impact on the practice of medicine than it does today. HMO managed care was in its infancy, and politicians only talked about the rapidly rising cost of healthcare's impact on the federal budget deficit. The general public was more trusting of doctors, less litigious, and less knowledgeable about information available on the Internet. The media was smaller and did not sensationalize or frighten the public as much about medical errors. In the past, doctors who exhibited aberrant behavior were considered eccentric, not persons engaging in behavior dangerous to patient care and patient safety.

Today, managed care is the dominant insurance in many states [15]. The 24/7 news media constantly inundates us with patient care horror stories occurring in hospitals, the more sensational the better. The government has imposed more regulations through HIPAA (the Health Insurance Portability & Accountability Act) and TJC (The Joint Commission), and patients use the Internet to study medicine and evaluate doctors and hospitals. The Institute of Medicine published a public report in 1999 that stated more than 90,000 patients die unnecessarily in hospitals every year because of mistakes made by doctors and nurses [5]. The report had wide media exposure, causing federal and state legislatures to provide even stronger regulation of doctors and hospitals.

Consequently, the triangular nexus between law medicine and politics is contributing to a more litigious environment for physicians in the daily practice of medicine. This environment is, as a result, hard wired within the triangle of law and medicine. The practice of medicine is no longer independent, distinct, and unattached to the other sides of the triangle. Much if not all that we do to provide care to patients is constantly monitored and evaluated by the public and those in the legal and legislative community. Consequently, it is imperative that physicians actively caring for patients be aware of the nature of the present healthcare environment. This awareness can be a significant factor in helping us to avoid medical malpractice and to eliminate disruptive behavior.

The dominant effect of this triangular nexus is the legalization of medicine. Documentation in the medical chart is no longer placing written information only for medical colleagues also treating the patient. Our documentation has become a financial and legal necessity for hospital reviewers so they can improve their organizations' reimbursement rate while simultaneously meeting state and federal requirements. Additionally, our documentation in the medical chart has become an absolute necessity for us to verify the quality of care we have given the patient. Thus, our progress notes must be focused, logical, and legible for third-party reviewers. In legal circles, it is sometimes suggested that it is not what you do but what you can prove. This shift in the burden of proof process is new for physicians, but it is a reality. As this legalization occurs, we physicians must become more knowledgeable about the law. We must adaptively move past our understandable emotions of anger, resentment, and frustration with all things legal. These negative emotions not only affect the care we give our patients but affect us physically, mentally, and spiritually. They influence our professional behavior. They influence our relationship with our family. These negative emotions contribute to the many stress-related morbidity and mortality illnesses we encounter as doctors [19]. Therefore, our ability to understand and adapt to this new healthcare environment paradigm shift is vital both personally and professionally.

THE MALPRACTICE MYTH

There are those, including some trial lawyers, who suggest that the idea of a medical malpractice crisis is not true. Tom Baker, in his book *The Medical Malpractice Myth*, concludes that the problem is too much medical malpractice not too many medical malpractice lawsuits [20]. He states in his book "Doctors are leaving the field of medicine, and those who remain are practicing in fear and silence…" "All this is because medical malpractice litigation is exploding. Egged on by greedy lawyers, plaintiffs sue at the drop of a hat. Juries award eye-popping sums to undeserving claimants, leaving doctors, hospitals, and their insurance companies no choice but to pay huge ransoms for release from the clutches of the so-called 'civil justice' system. Medical malpractice litigation is a sick joke, a roulette game rigged so that plaintiffs and their lawyers' numbers come up all too often, and doctors and the honest people who pay in the end always lose. This is the medical malpractice myth" [20].

Undoubtedly, what many fail to understand is that for physicians the problem is the entire process of malpractice litigation, not just those cases where malpractice has actually occurred. David Studdert and colleagues, in a recent review of 1452 malpractice lawsuits, reported in the May 2006 issue of *The New England Journal of Medicine* that in 40% of the lawsuits reviewed there was no evidence of medical error or verifiable injury. Nevertheless, in 16% of those cases, the patients received financial compensation [21]! It is this 40%, representing frivolous lawsuits with money-driven mentality, that makes dedicated physicians, both men and women, more defensive while providing patient care. Within this 40%, every time a physician is merely named in a lawsuit, his or her malpractice insurance rates increase. This increase will occur even if she or he is immediately dropped from the case; thus, frivolous malpractice lawsuits create a large financial burden for doctors. Furthermore, the time and financial pressure are just a part of the stress providers encounter. There is always an associated and a cumulative psychological and physical toll. These effects are both short term and long term. Admittedly, all share some blame for the highly charged litigious environment that exists. Dr. Kodner, a world-renowned surgical ethicist, in his chapter on ethical and legal considerations, noted "In recent decades, although we can technically and scientifically do more for our patients than ever before, our personal, trusting relationship with them has deteriorated to the point where it is sometimes adversarial. We have allowed medicine to become a business, guided in many cases by the financial bottom line, rather than by the uncompromising concern for a sick person." He went on to observe: "Within this fast-moving corporate system, we see too many patients, do too much surgery, and do not have time to develop a close mentoring relationship with our chosen role models, nor with our trainees. The cherished patient–physician relationship has been undermined by our own successful advances. Many of the operations that we do on a routine daily basis were not even imagined as possible only a few decades ago. Not only can we do more, but also our patients have come to expect perfection from us. Our society seems willing to accept flaws from many sources, but not from physicians and medical delivery systems. This situation is made even more complicated by a system in which individuals purchase their healthcare coverage when they are well and willing to buy the cheapest plan possible; but they utilize their coverage, especially for surgical problems, when they are sick and want the maximum that the system can deliver, without regard to time and cost. No individual has ever admitted that they purchased a cheaper plan, and thereby understood that only limited care should be provided to a loved one who is ill" [22].

We are all now being held more accountable for our actions. Previously, we were accountable primarily to our patients and ourselves. Society allowed us to independently review and police ourselves. Now society, for a variety of reasons as just noted above, has changed. The government is concerned about limited healthcare resources in the face of a fast-growing general population. Business is concerned about the constant rising cost of healthcare for their employees. And the public believes the quality of healthcare it receives in this country is far below what it should be and that far too many medical errors occur. As a result, physicians are being inundated with restrictive rules and laws. Increased litigation for physicians is a by-product of many of these changes.

THE SCIENCE OF LITIGATION

A new approach to decreasing the rate of malpractice litigation is called the science of litigation. It involves taking an evidence-based scientific approach to the malpractice liability problem [23]. The science of litigation is defined as the study of medical malpractice patterns using social science or scientific research methods. According to Dr. Frederick Greene, Chairman Department of General Surgery, Carolinas Medical Center: "Elevating medical malpractice and especially surgical malpractice issues to a true science is both timely and appropriate if proper prophylactic methodology is to be developed. The past approaches to malpractice issues that affect all of us as surgeons have dealt mainly with the analysis of claims and the reporting of economic consequences. We have been regaled by studies from both the defense and plaintiff's bar that has mainly been fodder for the foundation of tort reform. Unfortunately, this effort, especially on the federal level, has been relatively futile. The time for a new direction and for the introduction of science is upon us" [24].

As a result of this new approach, physicians are discovering that they are more in control of litigation issues than previously thought. For example, when a patient develops a wound infection after having surgery, we scientifically review the case and the appropriate literature and determine with our colleagues (morbidity and mortality conference or peer review meeting) how to prevent such postoperative infections in the future. The same approach is now being taken to decrease medical malpractice lawsuits. Instead of relying only on compensation issues and claim analysis, we now able to make a root cause analysis of exactly why the lawsuit occurred. Christina Frangou noted that the science of litigation has discovered four factors that have emerged from scientific evidence-based medicine reviews of malpractice suits [25]:

- Most lawsuits come from medical mistakes.
- Most mistakes most likely involve surgical patients.
- Providers who are poor communicators are sued most often.
- Hospitals and doctors who have documented their commitment to improving communication and decreasing medical mistakes are less likely to be sued.

A scientific approach brings an air of comfort and familiarity for physicians. Just as we review the evidence-based medicine for the best way to treat heart disease and lower cholesterol, we can also use an evidence-based approach to determine the most common reasons medical malpractice lawsuits occur. With this new empowerment, we have more direct control over the rate of new litigation. By taking more direct overall responsibility, we are more effective in influencing the outcome. In the tort reform approach, we must approach legislators (most of whom are lawyers), educate them about the problem, and then motivate them to seek a solution. It is understandable why there has been limited success with this approach. Therefore, a scientific evidence-based review of medical malpractice litigation will prove to be much more effective in nationally decreasing malpractice lawsuits than tort reform.

4

Definition of Malpractice: Negligence

Let's kill all the lawyers.
William Shakespeare

Medical malpractice falls under the legal division of tort law [1]. Tort means injury. There are many tort laws, but malpractice is in a unique tort law area called negligence [15]. Negligence says the surgeon acted unreasonably under the circumstances as he or she provided care for the patient. At the same time, the patient was injured, and the action of the surgeon caused the injury. Reasonableness is determined by what a similarly situated physician would do.

MALPRACTICE = NEGLIGENCE
- ■ Definition: Acting unreasonably under the circumstances
- ■ Reasonable refers to prudent physician standard of care
- ■ Unreasonable refers to acting below the standard of care

The law of **negligence** is different from **intent**. Negligence does not suggest the doctor did something intentionally or on purpose. Thus, intent is irrelevant. Negligence in essence says that something bad happened, that the doctor did it, and, based on training, knowledge, and experience, the doctor should have known better.

There are four elements to the tort law of negligence: duty, breach, causation, and damages. At issue initially is whether the doctor has a duty to the patient.

Duty is defined as the existence of a doctor–patient relationship [14]. The most common way a duty attaches is by mutual consent. Mutual consent is a contract law principle. In contract law, two parties each perform or promise to perform something that is of value to both parties. If one party fails to keep his promise, that party is in breach of their contractual responsibility and the aggrieved party may seek money damages in court as a remedy. Malpractice is similar. For example, a patient sees me in the office because of acute right lower quadrant abdominal pain at McBurney's point with rebound tenderness. The pain is associated with nausea, vomiting, elevated white blood cell count, and a low-grade fever. I agree (consent) to care for the patient. I do a through history and physical examination and a review of appropriate tests. I conclude the patient has acute appendicitis and needs emergency surgery. The patient agrees (consents). Therefore, we have developed a doctor–patient relationship based on mutual consent. Sometimes the consent may be implied. As an example, suppose I stop my car at the scene of an accident to help a passenger who is injured but unconscious and I render care. Although the patient is unconscious, consent on the patient's part is implied because the law presumes any injured patient would want to be helped. Can a patient whom I have helped at the scene of an accident successfully sue me while I am acting as a Good Samaritan doctor (no legal duty to help a stranger)? Many states have Good Samaritan laws to protect doctors and encourage us to help others. Nevertheless, patients can successfully sue if they can prove the doctor acted below the standard of care in a way determined to be grossly negligent or reckless (an exception to the Good Samaritan law). Also, most state Good Samaritan laws have a requirement of volunteerism. Therefore, if the provider sends the patient a bill later for treatment at the accident, the protective effect of the Good Samaritan may dissipate. Billing for services rendered is not volunteerism.

Many times a physician may have a duty to a patient without even knowing that she does. An example is third-party beneficiary. Third-party beneficiary is a contracts law concept also [14]. It says, in essence, if two parties agree to a contract that is to benefit a third party and one party breaches the contract between the original parties, resulting in injury to the third party, that third party has a right to sue the breaching party of the original two parties if he can prove damages. For example, many physicians in private practice are on call for their local hospital emergency room to cover patients who come to the emergency room but who do not have an assigned private physician [26]. If a physician is called on a scheduled on-call day to see an appropriate patient in the emergency room and refuses, and the patient has a bad outcome (damages), that emergency room patient may successfully sue the on-call doctor who refused to come, even though the on-call doctor never saw the patient. The on-call doctor had an agreement with the hospital to provide a service that would benefit any emergency room patient in his specialty area (third party). Because the doctor did not come when called, he breached his contractual obligation with the hospital (second party), therefore giving the third-party patient standing to sue, if the patient has injury (damages) caused by failure of the doctor to fulfill his contractual obligations (breach). The physician's duty has already been established by the patient's third-party beneficiary status [26].

Similarly, if I am a primary care physician who has signed a capitation agreement with an HMO (healthcare management organization), I have a contractual relationship with the HMO. Patients (third party) are randomly assigned to me with the understanding that they can see me for appropriate medical problems. As a primary care member of the HMO panel, I receive a monthly payment for each patient assigned to me whether I see the patient or not. If I refuse to see a patient on my list for an appropriate medical problem (breach) and, because I did not see the patient (causation), the patient has a bad outcome (damages), that patient may have standing to sue me as a third-party beneficiary to my contract with the HMO.

Above all, remember the doctor–patient relationship (duty) is a *relationship*. As with any relationship, it should be based on mutual respect and mutual trust. The physician should establish a rapport with the patient. The doctor should provide quality care that is consistent with the patient's reasonable expectations. Last, the physician should communicate effectively.

> ### DOCTOR–PATIENT RELATIONSHIP
> ■ Mutual consent
> ■ HMO
> ■ ER backup

Res ipsa loquitor is a more novel way the law may show that negligence has occurred. It is a unique legal term meaning "it speaks for itself" [15]. To imply duty for a presumption of negligence with this approach, only three elements need be met. First, it must be shown that the injury would not have occurred unless someone was negligent. Second, it must be shown that the defendant had exclusive control of the situation. Third, it must be shown that the patient did not contribute to the negligence. Therefore, there are many ways in which a physician can have a duty to a patient. Some are obvious and direct (mutual consent) and some are indirect [emergency room (ER) coverage, HMO assignment, etc.]. A physician who is able to recognize and understand when he or she has a duty fulfills his medical obligation; thus, he may be able to avoid unnecessary litigation.

To breach one's duty is to act below the Standard of Care. The essence of a successful malpractice case is for the plaintiff to prove that the physician has breached his duty of care to the patient; in other words, the doctor acted below the standard of care. Standard of care means action taken by another physician in the same situation. It is another area of legal grayness. Another physician, called an expert witness, who has knowledge and experience in the same clinical area will be asked to review the case and define the community standard of care. Acting below the standard of care is described as acting unreasonably under the circumstance and is, thus, a breach of the physician's duty to the patient.

> ### BREACH = UNREASONABLE ACTION

The patient's plaintiff attorney must show causation. The attorney must show that the unreasonable action of the doctor was the actual and proximate cause of the patient's injury. Usually, the facts will show the surgeon's action caused the injury. Therefore, causation is not in dispute in most malpractice cases.

Damages must have occurred [1,14]. Damages are usually described as pain and suffering and economic loss. Economic loss includes the loss of both wages and future earnings. Nationally, there have been attempts to place a limit on the amount recoverable by patients for pain and suffering in medical malpractice claims. Pain and suffering is a major factor in the high cost of malpractice insurance because its dollar value is more subjective and thus unlimited [26].

FOUR ELEMENTS OF NEGLIGENCE
- ◾ DUTY: Doctor–patient relationship
- ◾ BREACH
- ◾ CAUSATION
- ◾ DAMAGES

DOCUMENTATION: THE DOCTOR'S SWORD AND SHIELD

What you do is your first line of defense, what you document is your second line of defense.

In real estate, it is said the three most important words are location, location, location. In healthcare today, the three most important words are documentation, documentation, documentation. The simplest and most effective way for physicians to protect themselves against needless litigation is by using thorough documentation. Documentation is the best way for the physician to provide positive evidence (shade of gray) about what occurred and why. It is an effective shield to clarify the record. Documentation improves quality patient care. It also helps prevent physicians from violating various regulatory laws such as the Health Insurance Portability and Accountability Act, The Joint Commission rules, and various federal and state laws [27].

> ### WHY DOCUMENT?
> ■ Quality care
> ■ Litigation defense
> ■ Regulators: JCAHO, DHS, OIG

Documentation should occur especially in four specific areas: outpatient care, inpatient care, telephone communications, and medication orders. Evaluations of the patient in the office or hospital should be thoroughly documented in a clear logical format. Many physicians use the SOAP (subjective, objective, assessment, plan) format to clearly communicate their evaluation and treatment plan for the patient. If a dispute about patient care arises, the first step will be for claimant representatives to review the patient's chart.

> ### MEDICAL RECORD: Detailed Progress Notes
> ■ S.O.A.P or similar format
> ■ Informed consent/refusal discussion
> ■ Treatment plan/rationale
> ■ Follow-up necessary
> ■ Communication to patient

Sometimes this review alone will prevent unnecessary litigation by showing the physician clearly operated within the standard of care. Telephone communication should be thoroughly documented at the time to give a clear chronology of the patient's care and to remind the physician about the gravity of advice given over the telephone.

> ### TELEPHONE DOCUMENTATION
> ■ Abnormal test results
> ■ Symptoms
> ■ Medical advice
> ■ Risks
> ■ Prescriptions
> ■ Noncompliance

Finally, medication prescribed must be legibly documented in the patient's chart, whether inpatient or outpatient. Patient safety is a major issue for healthcare providers today. A very common patient safety problem is medication errors [28].

PRESCRIBING ERRORS
- Prescription orders illegible or unclear
- Prescription incomplete
- Drug name misspelled
- Trailing zero used as decimal (2.0)

Physicians should use verbal orders at a minimum, legibly communicate written orders, and avoid dangerous abbreviations such as U, IU, Q.D., QD, qd, QOD, Q.O.D., qod, MS, MSO_4, $MgSO_4$. We must time, date, and sign all our orders for them to be fully documented. In today's healthcare environment, if it is not documented, it is not done. Importantly, if the notes are not readable by a third party, the physician has not documented. Thus, if it is not legible, it is not documented. Legibility is a much more serious issue today than in the past [28].

LEGIBILITY

If a doctor notices he has made an error in the chart, he should simply draw a single line through the incorrect entry. After drawing the line, he should initial the line and write the correct entry in the chart. Never erase or remove a sheet from the chart: it is a "legal document." If legal issues were to develop with the patient, any changes in the chart, however innocent, could affect the doctor's credibility.

As noted earlier, the legalization of medicine has created greater importance for the medical record. That record is a legal document [29]. The record, because of increased physician accountability, has become an indispensable written vehicle to assure care was properly provided. This concern especially arises when there is a dispute between the patient and the physician.

Patient Safety

Patient safety is the elimination of medical mistakes. In 2004, The Joint Commission (TJC) made patient safety its top priority as a result of political and public pressure [30]. Patient safety is now equal to quality patient care as a national health standard. TJC initially evaluated sentinel event reports from its accredited hospitals. A sentinel event is defined as "an unexpected occurrence or variation involving death or serious physical or psychological injury, or the risk thereof." A sentinel event committee was formed, including representatives from leading national healthcare organizations. The Joint Commission's sentinel event committee then developed the national patient safety goals for all its hospitals and physicians. The most recent National Patient Safety Goals include requirements as follows [30]:

- Improve accuracy of patient identification
- Improve communication among caregivers
- Improve safety of medications
- Reduce risk of healthcare-acquired infections
- Reduce falls
- Reconcile medications throughout the continuum of care
- Reduce influenza and pneumococcal infections
- Decrease fires in operating rooms (ORs)
- Increase involvement of patient and patient's family with safety
- Decrease pressure ulcers

A major factor in the occurrence of medical errors is poor communication among members of the medical team. A common medical error is a verbal order or medication error. Communication is both verbal and written: doctors must use both clearly. Consequently, nurses are instructed to read back all verbal orders to ensure accurate communication. Physicians are instructed to eliminate various confusing abbreviations that can lead to medication mistakes with the patient. Another significant cause of medical errors in most hospitals is illegible physician handwriting. Various approaches have been tried to solve this problem, but most have had limited success. Reliable voice recognition software may be the ultimate answer to this challenging problem. Under the patient identification safety goal, The Joint Commission has mandated the universal protocol in surgery. The universal protocol is created to eliminate wrong-side/wrong-site, wrong-procedure, and wrong-person surgery. This protocol requires a preoperative verification process that includes a preoperative checklist, marking the operative site, and a time-out period before the incision.

It is vital that physicians be familiar with all aspects of the national patient safety goals. Compliance with the goals is a requirement for hospital accreditation. It is also a requirement for physician reappointment to the hospital medical staff, as mandated by The Joint Commission. These goals are rapidly approaching legal status as standard of care.

Documentation for Discontinuation of Patient Care

Sometimes the doctor–patient relationship needs to be terminated by the doctor [31]. Some reasons the doctor may desire to discontinue caring for the patient include the following:

- Patient is noncompliant
- Patient will not pay his or her bill
- Patient is an addict only seeking drugs
- Patient is abusive, harassing, or intimidating with physician and staff

It is important that, when the physician severs the doctor–patient relationship, it be done properly to avoid even the perception of patient abandonment. Abandonment is the termination of sufficient services without notice where a continuation of care is needed. The three elements needed to prove patient abandonment against the physician are the following [32]:

■ The termination was not by mutual consent but was a unilateral decision by the doctor
■ The termination occurred without reasonable notice
■ The termination occurred when continuous care was necessary

The most important of these elements is that concerning reasonable notice. Patients must have a reasonable amount of time to find another doctor. Thirty days has been suggested by some authorities. These are patients who are noncompliant, abusive, intimidating, or drug seeking, or who are just not following medical advice sufficiently. Your termination process of the patient should be done in writing in a nonacute care situation. You should remain available to the patient for 10 to 30 days and provide the patient with a list of a least three other qualified doctors in the area if possible. Consider notifying the patient in writing with a neutral, benign letter.

INFORMED CONSENT: A PROCESS NOT A FORM

Physicians have a right to inform, patients have a right to refuse

In 1990, Congress passed the Patient Self Determination Act. This federal law codified the principle that every competent adult patient has the right of self-determination [33]. It noted that all adult inpatients had to be given information about their rights under applicable state laws governing advance directives, including the following:

■ The right to participate in and direct their own healthcare decisions
■ The right to accept or refuse surgical or medical treatment
■ The right to prepare an advance directive
■ Information on the hospital's policies that govern these rights

The act also forbids discrimination by hospitals and other providers against patients who do not have an advance directive. This act codified the patient's rights of autonomy and legally ended the paternalistic approach to healthcare in this country.

Express and implied in this law is the right to be informed by the physician before consenting to any type of healthcare treatment. The duty to inform the patient is a fiduciary, nondelegable duty on the part of the doctor [34]. Many cases of medical malpractice involve some type of informed consent problem. Often informed consent is given but not properly documented. At issue is whether the patient received adequate information to agree to a type of treatment or procedure [15].

What Is Consent?

Consent is permission or approval. If a person is touched without consent (permission), it is a battery. If you put someone in fear of being touched without consent, it is an assault. Therefore, assault and battery are legally defined as unpermitted touching of another or the fear of unpermitted touching [35].

What Is Informed Consent?

Informed consent is defined as consent given by the patient based on sufficient information where the patient understands the nature of the procedure or treatment and the risks, benefits, and alternatives.

What Should Be Included in an Informed Consent?

The reasonable risks of the treatment or procedure should be explained in understandable terms. The benefits of the treatment or procedure need to be discussed. Finally, the alternatives to the proposed treatment or procedure, including doing nothing, must be included to complete the informed consent process.

INFORMED
- Benefits of treatment
- Risks of treatment
- Treatment alternatives

Who May Consent?

Only a competent patient can give informed consent. Competence in general is defined as a patient who understands the nature and consequences of the proposed treatment or procedure and can communicate his or her wishes to the physician. Because individual state definitions may vary, local statute or medical society definitions should be reviewed.

Can emergency medical treatment proceed without patient's consent [35]? Emergency treatment without consent is allowed under the following conditions:

- A physician or healthcare practitioner determines the patient is in need of immediate medical treatment.
- The patient is unable to consent because the patient is a minor or has a physical or mental impairment.
- No known surrogate of the patient is available to give consent.
- Delay in treatment would endanger the patient's life or health.
- The treatment is limited to that necessary to treat the emergency.
- There is no known evidence that the patient would oppose treatment.

Refusal of Treatment

A competent adult patient may refuse treatment for any reason at any time [35]. As already noted, only the doctor can give informed consent. Neither nurses nor hospital employees are capable of giving a patient informed consent about a treatment a physician will perform.

ONLY THE PHYSICIAN MAY GIVE INFORMED CONSENT

Additionally, the information must be of sufficient quality and in plain words and understandable by the patient. Reasonable risks of treatment, benefits of treatment, and alternative treatments are required elements of any informed consent process. Although most doctors verbally discuss these issues with patients before treatment, it is always better to have a written note in the chart, explaining risks, benefits, and alternative treatment. Patients may deny receiving or not remember they received certain information from the surgeon.

Documentation is again the key element of proof for physicians. Credibility of the doctor and patient is the essence of the informed consent issue. It is imperative that physicians obtain good informed consent that is appropriately documented. Remember, physicians have a duty to inform, patients have a right to refuse. This act alone may deter needless malpractice litigation.

DOCUMENTATION DEFENSE PROBLEMS
- Unclear informed consent/refusal
- No documentation of instruction
- No documentation of noncompliance
- Lack of physician treatment rationale
- No investigation of significant symptoms

THE ARBITRATION AGREEMENT: A PREEMPTIVE STRIKE?

Arbitration is an alternative to a jury trial. It is a dispute resolution process in which arbitrators hear both sides and render a binding agreement. Because malpractice issues are under the supervision of state law, the ability to use arbitration will vary with each state. Nevertheless, binding arbitration agreements can keep malpractice claims out of court and decrease the cost of a lawsuit for the patient and the physician. Some physicians believe just having the agreement in place serves as a deterrent to frivolous lawsuits. Arbitration agreements are contracts (agreements the court will enforce) that should be written by an attorney to assure their enforceability in court if challenged. Some state medical societies and regional professional malpractice liability carriers will provide free forms to their members [26,36].

ARBITRATION IS AN ALTERNATIVE

The agreement must state to the patient in plain English (or appropriate language)—not legalese—that he or she is knowingly waiving his or her right to a jury trial. It must also clearly communicate to the patient that arbitrators are neutral third parties with the ability to award any amount in money damages that the patient can receive in a court. Finally, the patient should understand the process of arbitration and the difference between a trial in court and a trial in front of arbitrators. Issues that should be included in an arbitration agreement include the following:

- How a demand is filed for arbitration
- Where the arbitration may be held
- How the arbitrator or members of the arbitration panel will be chosen
- What alternative dispute resolution organization will supply the chosen arbitrator
- Who pays for arbitration

Dr. Eric Shore notes, "Arbitration increases the likelihood that an attorney will accept their case, if it is valid. The average medical malpractice case cost from $20,000 to $60,000 to bring to trial and a trial could easily add another $25,000 to the tab. Most attorneys are reluctant to make that kind of investment even when liability is obvious, if the probability of winning a lucrative award is small" [37].

Trials have frequent delays, and may last 2 to 3 weeks, significantly disrupting one's practice. Trials are also a public forum; some jurors may be unsophisticated, and the verdicts are unpredictable. On the other hand, arbitration panel hearings are a private forum and usually last 2 to 3 days. The hearings are conveniently scheduled, evidence only is presented, and the results are predictable. Some have suggested that arbitration hearings result in 20% to 30% less in defense costs but that the amount awarded to patients is the same.

> ARBITRATION
> "The process of dispute resolution in which a neutral third party—an arbitrator—renders a decision after a hearing at which both parties have had an opportunity to be heard."

Our office has been using arbitration agreements for a number of years. Presently, we have not had any cases since our arbitration agreement has been in place. Whether this agreement will make a significant difference I do not know. However, I believe we are being proactive and this makes our entire staff feel more secure. An arbitration plan for your medical office is a way to educate each member of your office staff about the importance of teamwork and good communication. It further educates them how to mitigate potential litigious situations.

Many patients in private practice are seen only in the emergency room or as hospital inpatients. This situation usually occurs when the physician is asked to give a consult for a very ill patient or provides coverage for the emergency room. These patients may never come to the physician's office in person. Consequently, the office arbitration agreement may not be available for these patients. This difference is significant because it is often the sicker, in-hospital patients who may pursue litigation because they are unhappy with their care. Admittedly, arbitration agreements may not be embraced by all providers as a benefit. Nevertheless, they are used regularly and enthusiastically by many physicians and their offices.

DIVERSITY: A NEW EXPOSURE

Our Diversity Is Our Strength

Most physicians continue to treat a very diverse patient population. This diversity adds to the normal stress and anxiety within the doctor–patient relationship. The anxiety is most demonstrated in the communication process between doctors and patients. Many patients believe physicians do not spend enough time with them explaining procedures and answering questions. Most communication is nonverbal; therefore, it is not only important what we say as physicians, but how we say it. Our tone and body language may say much more to the patient and family than the words we use.

COMMUNICATION WITH PATIENTS IS MOSTLY NONVERBAL

Additionally, federal and state legislators are becoming increasingly concerned about quality healthcare disparities among various ethnic groups. The next legal wave of regulation for doctors and hospitals will be in the area of providing quality care that is also "culturally competent." The Department of Health and Human Services (HHS) now recommends 14 national federal standards for culturally and linguistically appropriate services in healthcare. In its report HHS noted, "National standards... respond to the need to ensure that all people entering the health care system receive equitable and effective treatment in a culturally and linguistically appropriate manner" [38].

These standards for culturally and linguistically appropriate services (CLAS) are proposed as a means to correct inequities that currently exist in the provision of health services and to make these services more responsive to the individual needs of all patients/consumers. The standards are intended to be inclusive of all cultures and not limited to any particular population group or sets of groups; however, they are especially designed to address the needs of racial, ethnic, and linguistic population groups that experience unequal access to health services. Ultimately, the aim of the standards is to "contribute to the elimination of racial and ethnic health disparities and to improve the health of all Americans." The 14 national federal CLAS standards are these:

- Healthcare organizations should ensure that patients/consumers receive, from all staff members, effective, understandable, and respectful care that is provided in a manner compatible with their cultural health beliefs and practices and preferred language.

- Healthcare organizations should implement strategies to recruit, retain, and promote at all levels of the organization a diverse staff and leadership that are representative of the demographic characteristics of the service area.
- Healthcare organizations should ensure that staff at all levels and across all disciplines receive ongoing education and training in culturally and linguistically appropriate service delivery.
- Healthcare organizations must offer and provide language assistance services, including bilingual staff and interpreter services, at no cost to each patient/consumer with limited English proficiency, at all points of contact in a timely manner during all hours of operation.
- Healthcare organizations must provide to patients/consumers in their preferred language both verbal and written notices informing them of their right to receive language assistance services.
- Healthcare organizations must assure the competence of language assistance provided to limited English-proficient patients/consumers by interpreters and bilingual staff. Family and friends should not be used to provide interpretation services (except on request by the patient/consumer).
- Healthcare organizations must make available easily understood patient-related materials and post signage in the language of the commonly encountered groups and/or groups represented in the service area.
- Healthcare organizations should develop, implement, and promote a written strategic plan that outlines clear goals, policies, operational plans, and management accountability/oversight mechanisms to provide culturally and linguistically appropriate services.
- Healthcare organizations should conduct initial and ongoing organizational self-assessments of CLAS-related activities and are encouraged to integrate cultural and linguistic competence-related measures into their internal audits, performance improvements programs, patient satisfaction assessments, and outcomes-based evaluations.

- Healthcare organizations should ensure that data on the individual patient's/consumer's race, ethnicity, and spoken and written language are collected in health records, integrated into the organization's management information systems, and periodically updated.

- Healthcare organizations should maintain a current demographic cultural and epidemiological profile of the community as well as a needs assessment to accurately plan for and implement services that respond to the cultural and linguistic characteristics of the service area.

- Healthcare organizations should develop participatory collaborative partnerships with communities and utilize a variety of formal and informal mechanisms to facilitate community and patient/consumer involvement in designing and implementing CLAS-related activities.

- Healthcare organizations should ensure that conflict and grievance resolution processes are culturally and linguistically sensitive and capable of identifying, preventing, and resolving cross-cultural conflicts or complaints by patients/consumers.

- Healthcare organizations are encouraged to regularly make available to the public information about their progress and successful innovations in implementing the CLAS standards and to provide public notice in their communities about the availability of this information [38].

The New Jersey Medical Board is the first state board to require proof of cultural competence education before receiving a license to practice medicine in the state [39]. More states are sure to follow because healthcare disparities continue to be viewed as a serious problem [40]. California and other states are asking physicians to voluntarily receive continuing medical education (CME) training in culturally competent care issues. Therefore, physicians must address diversity as a significant healthcare issue in practice and avoid another area of potential liability. Always remember, respect transcends all cultures. It is not necessary to be an expert on the specific uniqueness of each ethnic group.

RESPECT TRANSCENDS ALL CULTURES

5

Eliminating Disruptive Physician Behavior

The healthcare environment has dramatically changed. Physician behavior is a major national healthcare issue. Some idiosyncratic behavior that was once accepted will no longer be tolerated. We all agree that disruptive behavior should not occur. It decreases the quality of patient care and it has a negative effect on patient safety. The challenge is deciding exactly what behavior can be defined as "disruptive." Who should make the decision and when and how should it be made?

THE DEFINITION

When former Supreme Court Justice Potter Stewart was asked to define a particular activity, he noted he could not define it but he knew when he saw it [41]. A similar approach has been used by many hospitals and medical staffs about defining disruptive behavior. Another more legalistic approach has been to define disruptive behavior very broadly, such that any physician action can be construed as being disruptive. Neither approach is particularly helpful to physicians or medical teams. It is imperative that medical staff leaders and hospital administrators develop a definition that is acceptable to both. The American Medical Association has defined disruptive behaviors as follows: "A style of interaction between a physician, patients, family members, hospital personnel or others, that interferes with patient care" [42].

It may be difficult to understand what the phrase "a style of interaction" actually means. Admittedly, the medical staff may consider that the foregoing definition maybe too vague. Yearly, the state medical boards receive a number of complaints about disruptive physician behavior. Consequently, the national organization that represents state medical boards, called, the Federation of State Medical Boards has defined disruptive behavior as follows:

> *"Aberrant behavior manifested through personal interaction with physicians, hospital personnel, patients' family members, or others, which interferes with patient care or could reasonably be expected to interfere in the process of delivering quality care"* [43].

The descriptive term "aberrant" is more helpful in understanding exactly what constitutes disruptive behavior. I would add to the foregoing that disruptive physician behavior is aberrant behavior manifested through personal interaction with physicians, hospital personnel, patients' family members, or others, which significantly interferes with patient care or could reasonably be expected to interfere in the process of delivering quality care or patient safety. Definitions are important because they provide a framework that enables medical staff leaders to adequately provide peer review of fellow doctors. Although various members of the healthcare team may disagree on the definition of disruptive behavior, all agree that patterns are important. Therefore, the definition of disruptive behavior is usually dependent on three important elements. The first element is the degree of aberrant behavior. The second element is the frequency of aberrant behavior. The third element is the circumstance in which questionable conduct occurred. Admittedly, there are some types of aberrant behavior that are so egregious that the frequency and circumstance may be irrelevant. However, the majority of cases will require evaluation of all three elements. As a result, the patterns of a certain behavior are most important. Examples of behavior that may be considered aberrant are the following [44]:

- Threatening or abusive language
- Degrading or demeaning comments
- Profanity
- Threatening or intimidating physical conduct
- Public derogatory comments about others

■ Inappropriate medical record entries
■ Idiosyncratic demands on staff
■ Blaming others for adverse outcomes

Although some of the aforementioned behavior maybe considered harmless, the degree, frequency, and circumstance will determine whether it has reached the level of disruptive behavior.

Moreover, a clearer description of disruptive behavior is that it is the same as general harassment. General harassment is defined as "a course of conduct (verbal or nonverbal) directed at a specific person that causes substantial emotional distress in such person and serves no legitimate purpose." It is important to remember that harassment is viewed subjectively from the perspective of the victim. There are many forms of general harassment involving subjects of race, color, national origin, mental disability, physical disability, marital status, or sexual orientation.

The most commonly recognized type of harassment is sexual harassment. In the federal government, harassment is defined as "any conduct that has the purpose of unreasonably interfering with an individual's work performance or creating an intimidating, hostile, or offensive working environment." Sexual harassment is discrimination on the basis of sex and a violation of the Civil Rights Act of 1964 [7,15]. The types of sexual harassment are male or female, heterosexual or homosexual. There are two elements of sexual harassment, each of which can independently trigger the violation. One element is the tangible employment action element, which occurs when the plaintiff is propositioned with job promotion, or threatened with job termination or demotion, etc., in exchange for sexual favors or withholding same. Another element of sexual harassment is the hostile work environment element, which is the most difficult to evaluate because it is very broad. The plaintiff can merely be working in the area where a physician is having a conversation with another person. The plaintiff may then be offended by conversation the physician is having with another in the plaintiff's work area, and this may create a hostile work environment for the plaintiff. A hostile work environment is subjective from the plaintiff's perspective. Legally, sexual harassment is different from sexual misconduct [14]. Harassment occurs between the doctor and other colleagues or employees. Sexual misconduct occurs between the doctor and patient or patient family members.

The hospital is not the only location where disruptive behavior may occur. Aberrant behavior may also occur in the physician's private medical office. Medical office staff may tend to be younger and less educated than hospital staff. Moreover, the doctor's office atmosphere is more relaxed and the physician has more authority. Thus, the office atmosphere may be conducive to abusive behavior. We physicians must be careful that our behavior in our office is as professional with our private medical office staff as it is in the hospital.

THE PHYSICIAN WHISTLE-BLOWER

Whistle-blower laws were created to allow persons to report wrongdoing to various regulatory agencies without fear of retaliation. A number of states include physicians as a protected class in this legislation. On many occasions the doctor complains about a hospital system or employee that has injured her patient. The doctor is written up by the nurse or employee (incident report). The incident report may accuse the physician of disruptive behavior, resulting in a peer review investigation. The issue of the doctor's behavior may completely overshadow the more serious patient care or patient safety issue that upset the doctor in the first place. The State of California provides a "rebuttable presumption" of wrongdoing against the hospital entity or persons who knew the physician medical staff member filed a grievance or complaint if the alleged retaliation occurs within 120 days of filing of the grievance or complaint [45]. A rebuttable presumption means the law will presume retaliation is occurring against the doctor unless the hospital entity can show evidence to prove otherwise. Whistle-blower legislation is not in effect in every state; thus, physicians should check if they are protected. This legislation provides a needed balance to allow doctors to assure quality care and patient safety, without being exposed to sham peer reviews or hospital entity retaliations. All physicians should contact their local medical society to assure this legislation is in place at the state level [46,47].

The physician is the only true advocate for individual quality patient care in our healthcare delivery system. The nurses work for the hospital and must follow the system outlined by the hospital administration. We are the persons with the one-on-one relationship with the patient. We are the ones who directly provide care to the patient. We are the ones the patient and their families depend on to relieve suffering and resolve their illness. We are the ones morally, ethically, and legally held ultimately responsible when something goes wrong. Thus, we have a strong incentive to influence and supervise the healthcare system that cares for our patients [43]. Some of the system is in our control; much of the system is outside our control. It is this lack of control coupled with increased responsibility that leads to physician frustration [46]. The frustration can lead to aberrant behavior. The challenge for medical staff leaders doing peer review is to separate legitimate patient care concerns and circumstances from aberrant behavior that is not related to patient care. If a clinician has a behavioral problem, he or she should receive support and care in a confidential and respectful manner, as any patient would. Each hospital has a physician well-being committee that can be extremely helpful in assisting doctors with medical or psychological problems. We doctors are human and have the same mental and physical fragility as many of our patients. However, to minimize the perception of disruptive behavior in these situations, we need to remember that it is often not what we say but how we say it. As doctors, we still have a significant amount of authority in acute care hospitals, and it is important that we use this authority for the benefit of our patients.

THE PROCESS

Most hospitals use the incident reporting system to alert that a doctor has engaged in disruptive behavior. A physician does or says something and is written up by an observer, usually a nurse. The report may go to the hospital risk management department, the medical staff office, nursing office, or another administration office. These hospital departments will also receive patient complaint letters. The Joint Commission, which accredits hospitals, now requires that incident report information on physicians be reviewed on a regular basis to determine whether doctors should retain their privileges to treat patients in the hospital. Nevertheless, there are major flaws with the incident reporting process [47]. Arguably, most incident reports never rise to the level of disruptive behavior. The system is easily abused because frequently the doctor has no idea she or he has been written up in an incident report by a nurse or anyone else. The doctor usually never sees the report.

THE COST TO THE PHYSICIAN

If a physician is determined to have been engaging in disruptive behavior, this finding can exact a major price from the doctor both personally and professionally. Some of the personal price may be caused by the following determinations [7,15,44,48]:

- Violation of the Federal Civil Rights Law, a misdemeanor: doctor pays $ fine.
- Assault and battery: doctor pays $ damages.
- Intentional infliction of emotional distress: doctor pays $ damages.
- Criminal charges: possible jail sentence.

Some of the professional loss physicians may incur after determined to have engaged in disruptive behavior include the following:

- Reprimand in physician's medical staff file
- Loss of hospital privileges
- Report to the State Medical Board
- Report to the National Practitioner Data Bank
- Loss of medical license to practice

Neither the foregoing personal losses nor the professional losses are covered by the physician's routine medical malpractice insurance. The financial losses must be covered personally by the doctor. Therefore, it is clearly not worth the risk for any physician to purposely engage in disruptive physician behavior.

THE JOINT COMMISSION 2007 MEDICAL STAFF GUIDELINES

For years there has been interest by a variety of individuals involved in healthcare to connect quality patient care to physician behavior. Except for rare circumstances (egregious behavior), there are no evidence-based data to show that disruptive physicians are incompetent clinicians. Nevertheless, The Joint Commission (TJC) has, for the first time, codified behavioral guidelines to be used in evaluation of physician competence. Every 2 years doctors must receive peer review and hospital evaluation to determine if they are still competent to provide quality care to patients. The review includes a body of data that track mortality, morbidity, compliance with performance measures, compliance with state and federal laws, and complaints against the doctor for any reason. The commission has expanded the areas of general core competences from three to six. The new areas—interpersonal and communication skills, professionalism, and system-based practice—are behavioral, not clinical [30]. The majority of these new evaluations will be vague and very subjective. It is important for the medical staff leaders to work with hospital and nursing administrators to develop a clear consensus on the interpretation of these criteria and how they can most appropriately be applied to physicians. The approach by the leaders should be collaborative not confrontational. Indeed, the accreditation agency has mandated that hospitals provide additional resources to implement these changes or the hospitals will be disciplined and could lose their accreditation.

SIX AREAS OF GENERAL COMPETENCE 2007
- Patient Care
- Medical and Clinical Knowledge
- Practice-based Learning
- Interpersonal and Communication Skills
- Professionalism
- System-based Practice

6

Pain Management: The New Legal Trojan Horse

Pain is a subjective symptom and varies with each individual patient. Pain can be either acute or chronic. Acute pain (nociceptive) is usually associated with an area of injury [49]. It arises from a stimulus outside the nervous system and is associated with increased autonomic activity. The pain is primarily limited to the injured area. When the injured tissue heals, the pain resolves. Acute pain serves a protective function for the body. The most common class of nonnarcotic medication used to treat acute pain is nonsteroidal antiinflammatory drugs (NSAIDs). They are divided into two categories: non-selective NSAIDs and selective NSAIDs. Nonselective NSAIDs block both enzymes cyclooxygenase 1 and cyclooxygenase 2. They are most effective for treating mild and moderate pain; their most serious complications include gastrointestinal bleeding and cardiac thromboembolic episodes. On the other hand, selective NSAIDs block only the cyclooxygenase 2 enzyme. The selective NSAIDs provide very good pain relief for mild, moderate, and severe pain. Their most serious complications are cardiovascular [50].

Chronic pain (neuropathic) occurs for at least a year and presents a different challenge [50]. It is not usually associated with a history or area of injury but is caused by a dysfunction of the nervous system. It can occur in areas of the body that are completely normal on physical examination. Example, a patient complains of severe foot pain, but on examination the foot appears completely normal. However, when the doctor touches the foot the patient screams in agony. This is a condition called allodynia and is common in some patients with chronic neuropathic-type pain.

Chronic pain can last indefinitely. As a result, it is often associated with anxiety and depression. Chronic pain does not have a protective function for the body. The treatment of acute and especially chronic pain can be very challenging for doctors. The physician must select the most appropriate pain medication for the patient and document that the patient has been made aware of potential complications of the medication.

Consequently, because of the medicine-legal-public triangle, surgeons have a new area of potential liability exposure. This exposure is based on the premise held by many persons that we physicians routinely undertreat hospitalized patients with pain medication. Therefore, a number of state legislators have passed laws to guarantee patients receive adequate pain management as a requirement of quality care. As an example, the State of California recently passed the Elder Abuse Act [51]. Patients seeking remedies under this act can be "elder," that is, a person 65 years of age or older, or a dependent adult. A dependent adult is defined by the act as any person between the ages of 18 and 64 years who is admitted as an inpatient to a licensed 24-hour health facility, or resides in California, and has physical or mental limitations that restrict his or her ability to carry out normal activities…. The California Supreme Court has held that "neglect" under this law does not necessarily refer to "the substandard performance of medical services, but rather, to the failure of those responsible for attending to the basic needs and comforts of elderly or dependent adults…to carry out their custodial obligations." Deprivation of goods and services that are necessary to avoid physical harm or mental suffering, such as adequate pain medicine, may constitute abuse. Moreover, cases are now being brought more frequently against physicians under the California Elder and Dependent Abuse Act [51]. Thus, it is very important for doctors to document in the medical record that the patient has received appropriate pain medication.

PAIN MANAGEMENT

- Fifth vital sign requirement for hospitals
- Twelve Continuing Medical Education credits (CME) by 2006 requirement for physicians
- Elder abuse
- Adult dependent abuse

The Joint Commission for the Accreditation of Healthcare Organizations (JCAHO) has demanded strict guidelines for the pain management of hospitalized patients [52]. If a hospital loses its JCAHO accreditation, it is not allowed to treat Medicare patients and is thus put in financial jeopardy. These guidelines also include a pain communication scale from 1 to 10 to help the physician and nurses more adequately assess the pain patients are experiencing.

In those states with these types of pain management laws, not providing adequate pain treatment, based on the physician's documentation, exposes doctors to a new area of needless litigation for elder abuse or dependent adult abuse. Remember, a dependent adult is any adult admitted to the hospital. Because elder abuse and dependent adult abuse claims are intentional torts (not negligence), they are not covered by routine malpractice insurance. Again, it is imperative to document why a patient is given a particular amount or type of pain medicine to prove the treatment provided is adequate.

7
Medical Informatics

Medical informatics is the use of computer-based technology with information management to provide patient care. We physicians have embraced many areas of computer technology but have been slow to apply our technology-based information management skills in the care of our patients. There are many reasons physicians have been reluctant to fully use the technology for patients, in spite of the laudable claims by politicians, the media, and various organizations [53]. First, as doctors we are trained to take a scientifically verifiable approach to any new process that affects our patients. From our journal clubs in residency training, we learned that every exciting claim is not what it appears to be. Facts and conclusions are not always true just because they were published in a journal or printed in a popular newspaper. Today our scientific approach is made even more difficult because of direct-to-consumer advertising by various healthcare vendors. As clinicians, we have a moral, ethical, and legal obligation to our patients to filter through the hype. We must carefully determine which programs, medications, and devices really improve patient care and patient safety [54]. Consequently, this deliberate approach is frequently misunderstood by many in the healthcare arena who do not understand why every doctor does not have an electronic medical record in his or her office. The medical informatics pressure on physicians will intensify in the near future. Financial cost is the second major reason for the average physician's reluctance to fully adopt technology-based information management systems [55]. Doctors have seen a yearly decline in their reimbursement for patient services during the past decade. This financial decline has been combined with a loss of control in a healthcare environment that is highly regulated and dominated by managed care. There must be stronger incentives for physicians to increase their involvement [56].

CYBERMEDICINE LEGAL ISSUES

Healthcare in cyberspace is more common with widespread use of the Internet to manage and treat a patient's medical problems [57]. A growing number of physicians are using web-based computer technology to treat patients in virtual medical offices. Cybermedicine is defined as the Internet-driven practice of medicine wherein the patient and the doctor communicate through electronic mail. This process of cybermedicine brings a unique array of medical legal issues. The issues can be divided into general corporate liability issues and physician practice liability issues.

General Corporate Liability

Corporate liability issues tend to involve hospitals and physicians as an entity. The most common areas of legal issues raised in cybermedicine are the following:

- Web-based marketing by healthcare organizations
- Web-based marketing and product support by pharmaceutical companies and manufacturers
- Health-oriented interactive advice sites by physicians and other providers

Many doctors' offices now have websites either individually or by affiliation with a hospital or medical group. A basic passive website may not add significantly to a clinician's liability exposure, providing the information on the site is truthful and accurate. However, when the site becomes more interactive with the potential patient, the doctor's liability exposure may increase.

A number of the cybermedicine cases so far have revolved around the issue of agency and corporate liability. Hospitals, similar to other corporations, may be liable under the doctrine of respondeat superior. This common law doctrine notes that an employer may be held liable for the negligent acts of omission of its employee, if said employee is acting within the course and scope of his or her employment [14,15]. At issue in malpractice cases is whether a physician provider is an agent (employee) of the hospital or an independent contractor. If the provider is deemed to be an independent contractor, the hospital has no corporate liability. Nevertheless, to protect the public, there is also a legal principle called apparent agency. This principle notes that an agent is one deemed to have whatever power or authority a person would reasonably infer, either from the principal's (employer's) representations concerning an agents (employee's) authority or from the agent's holding himself out as having proper authority; thus, the corporation may be obligated as if it had expressly granted the authority to the agent. Consequently, a patient does not need to prove a physician is a definite employee of the hospital to find the hospital corporately liable in a malpractice case. The patient only has to prove it reasonable to infer the provider is employed by the hospital based on actions and representations made by the hospital or the physician. One of these representations is the increasingly sophisticated marketing by hospitals and providers on the Internet. Much of this cyberspace activity makes it easier for patients to claim a reasonable reliance on the belief that the doctor works for the hospital and that the hospital is ultimately responsible for the doctor's actions.

In the case Kashishian v. Port, plaintiff wanted to make the hospital liable for the alleged negligence of a cardiologist who was not employed by the hospital [57]. The patient used the theory of apparent agency. The court expanded the institutional liability beyond narrow fact patterns of hospital departments by stressing the marketing endeavors of the hospital corporation by stating:

> "Cases and commentaries on the doctrine invariably point to the recognition that hospitals increasingly hold themselves out to the public in expensive advertising campaigns as offering and rendering quality health care services. One need only pick up a daily newspaper to see full and half page advertisements extolling the medical virtues of an individual hospital and the quality health care that the hospital is prepared

to deliver in any number of medical areas. Modern hospitals have spent billions of dollars marketing themselves, nurturing the image with the consuming public that they are full-care modern health facilities.

All of these expenditures have but one purpose: to persuade those in need of medical services to obtain those services at a specific hospital. In essence, hospitals have become big business, competing with each other for health care dollars. As the role of the modern hospital has evolved, and as the image of the modern hospital has evolved (much of it self-induced), so too has the law with respect to the hospital's responsibility and liability towards those it successfully beckons. Hospitals not only employ physicians, surgeons, nurses and other health care workers, they also appoint physicians and surgeons to their hospital staff as independent contractors. What is the responsibility of hospitals when these independent contractors render negligent health care? Can they escape liability for the rendering of negligent health care in all instances simply because the person rendering the care was an independent contractor, regardless of how hospitals held themselves out to the consuming public, regardless of how the doctor rendering the health care held himself or herself out to the consuming public, and regardless of the perception created in the mind of the consuming public? We think not" [57].

In Sword v. NKC Hospitals, Inc., the plaintiff attempted to hold the hospital liable on an apparent agency theory [14,15,57]. Plaintiff alleged negligence on the part of an anesthesiologist who was not a hospital employee. That court held as follows:

"For a hospital to be held liable for the negligence of a health care professional under the doctrine of apparent agency, a plaintiff must show that the hospital acted or communicated directly or indirectly to a patient in such a manner that would lead a reasonable person to conclude that the health care professional who was alleged to be negligent was an employee or agent for the hospital, and that the plaintiff justifiably acted in reliance upon conduct of the hospital consistent with ordinary care and prudence."

The Sword court found in favor of the plaintiff because of the defendant's external marketing activity. The provider's web activity in a growing number of jurisdictions appears to increase liability based on respondeat superior, or institutional medicine's corporate liability.

Physician Practice Liability

Cybermedicine is a new area of the law that is still in its infancy. In contrast to corporate liability, success against individual doctors can be challenging for the average plaintiff because the patient will need to show foreseeable injury on the part of the defendant provider. Traditionally, the practice of medicine involves physically seeing the patient, taking a medical history, and doing an appropriate physical examination. In cybermedicine, the doctor interacts with the patient only through e-mail. Patients like it because it is less expensive and they do not have to wait for an appointment. Nevertheless, the American Medical Association has raised concerns about the quality of care given to the patient. It is not considered standard of care to evaluate patients and prescribe their treatment without doing an appropriate physical examination. The major legal issues have centered on prescribing medication over the Internet. Internet prescribing occurs in three areas:

- Online sale of medication to patients with a prescription from a local doctor
- Online sale of medication to patients with a prescription after online consultation only
- Online sale of medication to patients without a prescription

The latter two areas cause the most legal difficulty. Lack of a verifiable physical examination is the main problem. Some patients may misrepresent their symptoms online just to get drugs. If there is no examination, the provider cannot verify that the patient is telling the truth. Physician credentialing is another major legal issue with cybermedicine. In hospitals and other healthcare organizations where physicians treat patients, the providers' credentials are verified to document that the doctor is who he says he is and that his stated credentials are true. The Joint Commission, which accredits healthcare organizations, mandates all physicians be thoroughly credentialed. Presently, in cybermedicine, there is no good way to credential providers and document that the people who say they are doctors on line really are qualified physicians.

Nevertheless, this is a dynamic legal area that continues to grow. Attorneys are rewarded for their creativity in finding new theories to bring litigation. Physicians need to be careful interacting with potential patients in cyberspace.

21ST CENTURY COMMUNICATION REQUIRES CAUTION

A frequent criticism of lawyers is that they never give a straight answer when asked a legal question. The reply to a legal query frequently is "it depends." This vagueness in communication is often viewed as a lack of complete honesty. Nevertheless, attorneys know that every answer to a legal question does "depend" on the facts of the case. To address a legal query completely, an attorney must understand the unique issues that depend on the unique facts of that situation. As physicians, we take pride in answering questions clearly and directly. We view this forthrightness not only as an issue of integrity but as intelligence and compassion for the person asking the medical question. In today's changing society, physicians must be cautious when replying to medical questions, especially in nontraditional venues [15]. A vague legal approach can be very useful on occasions.

Social Communication

When in a social setting outside the office or hospital, we like to relax and forget about medicine. Invariably, someone who has just learned you are a doctor will ask a question for medical advice. Be careful and remember the lawyer's approach. Be vague in your answer.

The issue is when does the doctor–patient relationship begin? The initiation of the doctor–patient relationship creates a duty on the part of the physician to the patient. Once a duty is created, the doctor's medical–legal contractual obligations attach. Remember the initiation of the doc-tor–patient relationship can occur at any time regardless of the location. Always advise the persons to seek definitive advice from their own physician, or ask the patient to see you formally should you choose to take the case.

PROCEED WITH CAUTION WITH:
- ■ "Curbside consults"
- ■ Q and A chat settings
- ■ Medical practice websites
- ■ Patient e-mail

Telephone Communication

As practitioners, we frequently get telephone calls from patients who want medication or want medical advice about vague symptoms. Keep a record of medication pre-scribed, especially after hours and on weekends. Follow legal guidelines: federal and most state laws require a "good faith exam" before giving prescribed medication for a new patient. Caution again is key when giving telephone advice. When communicating with patients on the telephone, always offer to see them in the office or suggest they go to the emergency room. I have found that by merely suggest-ing patients go to the emergency room I can get an idea about how serious they believe their symptoms really are. The best medical treatment occurs after a thorough his-tory and good physical examination. A patient's unilateral description to you over the phone about their symptoms is neither. Resist the temptation to definitively treat patients over the telephone.

E-Mail and Internet Communication

Society as a whole now communicates more frequently via the Internet [53,58]. Younger physicians (less than 40 years of age) are more comfortable with communication via e-mail or text messaging. Many patients want to com-municate with their doctor directly via e-mail. This form of doctor–patient communication bypasses the normal protective filter of the medical office staff or medical answering service. A virtual medical practice is a nice concept but may not always be the most reasonable way for physicians to practice quality medical care and patient safety.

Cybermedicine is still in an infant stage medically. The primary medical–legal issues are responding in a timely manner and, as already noted, not doing a good physical examination. Therefore, physicians should avoid giving definitive medical advice for any new condition or for a new patient. Never give definitive medical advice and treatment to patients in another state whom you have never met or examined. Most states have laws to discourage and punish physician from treating patients in a state where they are not licensed.

E-MAIL

- ■ Have a patient education sheet
- ■ Timeliness response
- ■ Who has access?
- ■ Determine acceptable communication

8

How to Say "I'm Sorry" Without Admitting Guilt

To err is human, to forgive Divine.

In spite of the honor roll grades in high school, the academic awards in college, the Medical College Aptitude Test (MCAT), the academic distinction in medical school, internship, residency, and fellowship, we will still make mistakes. And sometime stuff really does just happen [5]. As physicians we pride ourselves in being thorough, intelligent, and compassionate. We have little tolerance for errors committed by members of our team or ourselves. We are devastated when things go wrong [59]. To prevent mistakes, we try to control the environment and members working with us. Nevertheless, errors would occur even if we could control everything and everybody. There are simply too many variables involved with the care of patients. As we experience these feelings of frustration, anger, denial, etc., we must be extremely careful how we act with patients or the patient's family, immediately after an unintended consequence [60]. It is okay to say "I'm sorry."[61] The doctor should explain the facts, listen to the patient or family, document the discussion in the chart, and stay in contact. We should not immediately blame others, avoid the patient's family, lie, lose control, or use negligent words [62]. We should be honestly empathetic and supportive. As with many potential litigious situations, it is not only what we say but how we say it.

FULL DISCLOSURE PROGRAMS: PROCEED WITH CAUTION

There are a number of full disclosure programs purported by hospital systems and other organizations. There stated objectives include making patients happier, teaching doctors how to admit mistakes, and significantly decreasing litigation trial cost for hospitals. Many investigators have offered reasons why doctors don't always publicly admit their medical errors. Mattow, from the Hospital of Sick Children in Toronto, recommends the following seven "W's" of disclosure [63].

Why disclose?

■ To preserve autonomy and patient–physician trust.
■ Because ethically it is the right thing to do.

Who should disclose?

■ Healthcare worker with whom the patient has a trusting relationship, usually the responsible physician.
■ Others involved in the incident (e.g., nurse, pharmacist may be included).
■ If the physician cannot disclose, another healthcare worker with an established relationship with the patient or a member of the hospital leadership or quality and safety program should do the disclosure.
■ A senior hospital administrator may need to be involved in serious cases.
■ The patient's primary nurse should be included in the discussions to be able to support the patient after the disclosure has occurred.

To whom should the communication be made?

■ To the patient.
■ If this is not possible, to family members or substitute decision makers.

What types of events should be communicated?

■ Any incident that has resulted in harm to the patient.
■ Other incidents at the discretion of the responsible physician.

What information should be communicated?

■ Acknowledge that the event occurred and give the facts.
■ Take responsibility and apologize.

- Commit to finding out why.
- Explain what impact the event will have on the patient now and in the future.
- Describe steps being taken to mitigate the effects of the injury.
- Describe steps being taken to prevent a recurrence.

When should communication take place?

- As soon as the event is recognized and the patient is physically and emotionally capable.
- Ideally within 24 hours after the event is recognized.
- Ongoing communication will be required as more information becomes available and should be led by the responsible physician or delegate.

Where should the communication take place?

- In a private and quiet area.

The fact is that physicians admit medical mistakes daily throughout the country in the peer review process. Peer review is a Joint Commission-accredited process where doctors closely scrutinize the actions of other doctors and make corrective action toward the doctor when warranted [30]. Peer review proceedings are not open to the public. They are protected from litigation to allow open communication to improve patient care. Although it is laudable to have full disclosure programs, physicians need to approach these hospital programs with caution. Physicians in private practice are independent contractors who care for their patients in their office, in outpatient centers, and in hospitals. We are not hospital employees and are not covered by the hospital's malpractice insurance. We must purchase our own malpractice insurance at rates that continually increase.

When major medical errors occur, they are caused by either the doctor or the hospital staff. Recognition of this doctor–hospital staff duality is an important but often missing element in many of these full disclosure hospital programs. Many physicians strongly supportive of these programs are in administration or academics, not the real world of private medical practice. The reality is that when there is a high probability of malpractice litigation, the hospital risk management department will notify the hospital attorney. Thus, it is imperative that physicians continue to similarly notify their private malpractice attorney before making any statements that can be used against them in court. In a highly emotional environment when death or serious bodily injury has occurred, the doctor's attorney is the only friend the doctor has in the room. On the other side, the hospital staff is represented by a multimillion dollar corporation that has a marketing/communication team, a risk management team, and a team of liability attorneys. The reality is there are times when the physician's interest and the hospital's interest may be adversarial. Oftentimes the physician may not recognize this adversity without first having a discussion with her or his legal counsel. All would agree its best to be completely open with patients; nevertheless, it is not a perfect world. Physicians must always get legal advice before making statements beyond "I'm sorry."

"I'M SORRY"

"I feel awful about what happened, but without a doubt, everyone did their best."

"I know that you are shocked, scared, and probably angry. That's perfectly natural."

"As we discussed before your surgery, these complication do sometimes occur. Let me explain what we plan to do."

WHAT PHYSICIANS CAN SAY

As just noted, an unlimited full detailed discussion during the emotion of the moment, after an error resulting in death or serious bodily injury, is not always legally in the best interest of the doctor. Nevertheless, it is important for physicians to talk about these occurrences. At issue is to whom you can talk and when. It is okay to talk in confidence to members of your support system: spouse, family, very close friend. It is probably alright to speak to a trusted colleague in confidence (make sure your attorney agrees). However, be very careful about speaking to anyone else about the case in detail unless it is in a legally protected peer review committee meeting. A peer review committee is usually one that is established as part of the medical staff structure and outlined in the medical staff bylaws [18]. Alternatively, it can be an ad hoc peer review committee appointed by the clinical department chair, medical executive committee, or the president of the medical staff. It will have a physician chair, and the majority if not all of the members will be doctors. Dr. Sara Charles, a professor of psychiatry at the University of Illinois College of Medicine, noted "Many attorneys and insurers understand that an absolute prohibition of any discussion of an event that becomes a legal case contradicts a person's need to talk about the overwhelming emotional disruption caused by one of the most serious experiences of their lives. Attorneys and insurers may also realize that suppressing these feelings may harm a person's health and ability to function. Physicians may resolve this chronic dilemma by accepting the implied discipline: They can talk about their 'feeling' regarding the event but not about the specifics of the event itself. Physicians can respect the concern of legal counsel and still choose to talk about the problem with a trustworthy and understanding confidant, sharing their overall reactions and mentioning specifics incidentally, if at all. Humans cannot avoid any talk about their reactions to a fatal event without mentioning anything about the nature of what happened. Physicians can, however, accept a literal interpretation by not discussing the specific facts of the case while still expressing their feelings about them" [64].

It is not only helpful but therapeutic for the physician to discuss the case providing this discussion occurs in the proper environment. It is important not to oversimplify these cases because clearly one size does not fit all. When a physician feels uncomfortable with the doctor–patient relationship, it is sometimes a warning of future litigation. Keep a personal record of the patient separate from the regular patient medical record. The personal record can be a single sheet of paper with treatment dates and any patient compliance issues. Personal records are usually not discoverable. If litigation does develop, it will be years later. Your personal notes will be invaluable for you and your defense team.

KEEP PERSONAL RECORDS

■ Differs from medical record
■ Not discoverable
■ Litigation may occur years later, so this is a good resource
■ Follow your instincts

9

You Have Been Served—
Now What?

First, take a deep breath and relax. Your life and career have not ended in spite of the emotions you are presently experiencing. You have probably just received a letter of intent from the patient's attorney. Read the letter, then immediately call your medical malpractice insurance carrier. Your malpractice carrier team will take you through the process step by step.

PHYSICIAN DOs

- Contact an attorney
- Save all records
- Write a summary of events and keep in a separate place from other documents
- Document thoroughly

Do not talk about the case to anybody you do not know. There are occasions when opposing attorneys may have someone call your office to get information about the case that may later be used against you. Do not ever attempt to change any records after the fact. Alteration of the medical record is always a bad idea. Although alterations need not involve a doctor's intent to deceive, it may destroy your credibility and your planned defense. Frequently, by the time the physician is aware of pending malpractice litigation, the plaintiff's attorney has subpoenaed a complete copy of the original medical records months earlier. Thus, any change from the original record will be immediately noticed. Additionally, there are professional handwriting analysts who can evaluate ink to determine the timing of an entry, whether the same pen was used, or whether pages have been removed from the original medical record. If you intentionally change a record it may be considered fraud (misrepresentation of a material fact) and disqualify you from representation from your own malpractice insurance company. Perception is reality and changing the medical record creates a perception of deception. Do *not* change the record. It is permissible to add an addendum to the record. Clearly state it is an addendum, and date, time, and sign on the date entered (do not backdate).

PHYSICIAN DON'Ts
- Don't talk to anyone about the case
- Don't alter any records
- Don't attempt to hide anything

Second, remind yourself that you are still a good person and a good doctor. You have been caught in a medical–legal web in caring for a difficult patient or you have made an error in clinical judgment. If you have erred, remember, to err really is human. Nevertheless, your spouse will still hug you and your kids will still want to play with you.

Third, remember to work with and trust the medical malpractice legal team you have been paying for through your malpractice premiums. Most malpractice claims are withdrawn or settled before they go to trial. If the case goes to trial, it will be 1 to 2 years after the initial filing. However, if it goes to trial, doctors usually win the case. Past circumstances and actions are now no longer in your control: focus on the future. Life really is too short not to enjoy it!

A FEW TERMS YOU SHOULD KNOW

Knowing some basic legal terms will make you feel less like an outsider. Table 9.1 is a 20-second lexicon that will get you through most of the legal settings you will encounter.

TABLE 9.1. Useful legal terms

Term	Definition or meaning
Plaintiff(s)	The person(s) bringing the lawsuit against you. It may be the patient, the patient's family, or a legal guardian.
Defendant(s)	The party or parties against whom the lawsuit is brought. There may be many defendants, and defendants can include hospitals, clinics, or laboratories, and anyone who was involved in the plaintiff's case.
Discovery	A pre-trial phase of a suit when both sides must disclose relevant facts, documents, and other evidence. The objectives are to locate evidence, preserve testimony, narrow issues, and remove surprises.
Direct examination	Initial questioning of a witness by the attorney who called the witness. Usually this is followed by the cross-examination and redirect examination.
Cross-examination	Questioning of a witness by a lawyer other than the one who called the witness about matters to which he or she testified in direct examination.
Redirect examination	Questioning of a witness by the attorney who originally called the witness after she or he has been cross-examined.
Adverse witness	Whenever counsel for either side calls an opposing party to the stand, the witness is "adverse." For example, if the plaintiff's attorney calls you to the stand while presenting his or her case, you are considered adverse, or "against" the plaintiff. This strategy is being used more and more.
Testimony	Any questioning done under oath that is recorded or transcribed.

(continued)

TABLE 9.1. (continued)

Term	Definition or meaning
Motion	An oral or written request made to the judge by an attorney regarding a legal rule or order.
Objection	Made whenever either attorney asserts that a witness, line of questioning, or piece of evidence is improper and should not be continued, then asks the judge to decide. If there is an objection during a deposition, you may be required to answer the question anyway, and it will be ruled on later at trial.
Complaint	The first pleading of the plaintiff(s), setting out their facts and allegations.
Interrogatories	A pre-trial discovery tool in which written questions are submitted to opposing side and to which a written reply, under oath, must be made. Interrogatories are often the first step in establishing facts known by defendants.
Deposition	A pre-trial discovery tool in which a witness is cross-examined under oath by opposing counsel, all of which is transcribed. A deposition may be taken of any witness, and it may be videotaped.
Reasonable medical certainty	The legal measure of probability meaning "more likely than not." It can also mean a "preponderance (51%) of the evidence" or that the amount of evidence is slightly more weighted on one side than the other. It does not mean absolute certainty.
Standard of care	Standards of behavior on which the theory of negligence is based. It requires the "actor" to do what a "reasonable person or ordinary prudence" would do in the actor's place. In medicine, the standard of care is that of a "reasonably competent physician in that specialty."

WHAT YOUR MEDICAL MALPRACTICE INSURANCE DOES NOT COVER

Malpractice insurance does not cover intentional torts (something done on purpose). Your insurance covers only tort injuries caused by negligence (what you should have done). It is very important for physicians to understand the limitation of malpractice insurance. Moreover, we physicians have liability exposure in a number of areas not covered by our insurance: some are listed next.

Elder Abuse and Dependent Adult Abuse: As noted earlier, intentionally undermedicating adult inpatients, without appropriated documentation, maybe considered abuse of those patients. If the doctor is found liable, he is not protected because intentional torts are not usually covered by malpractice insurance.

Sexual Misconduct: Inappropriate behavior of a sexual nature with a patient is not covered under malpractice insurance.

Sexual Harassment: It is defined as any conduct that has ... "the purpose of unreasonably interfering with an individual's work performance, or creating and intimidating, hostile, or offensive work environment."

Assault and Battery: A battery occurs when a person is touched without permission. Assault occurs when a person is afraid that a battery will occur. Because these are intentional torts, they are not covered by regular medical malpractice insurance.

As physicians we must realize the law is not static but a dynamic entity. It is constantly changing, growing, and seeking new areas to influence. This dynamic activity exists because lawyers and legislators are rewarded for their creativity. The more creative ways the law can be used and applied, the better it is for them. The types of intentional tort injuries just listed occur more than they should. Physicians found responsible for any of the aforementioned intentional torts are be financially liable, and malpractice insurance will not cover the loss.

10

Basic Steps in a Medical Malpractice Lawsuit

Most cases proceed through the same basic steps, although every malpractice lawsuit is unique. It takes approximately 2 to 3 years to get through the complete legal process. However, a case may be dismissed or settled before going to trial, and most are. If a suit is not dismissed or settled, the defendant physician will be involved in the following steps:

1. A complaint is filed by the plaintiff(s), the person(s) bringing the lawsuit. You will receive a letter of intent to sue or another form of legal notification. This notification may be your first indication that a claim is being filed against you.

2. You immediately notify your malpractice insurance company. Your company hires a defense attorney. He or she contacts you and discusses the case. He then responds to the written complaint against you. Your company may also hire expert physician consultants to review your case and advise them about the strengths and weaknesses of the lawsuit.

3. The discovery phase begins. Discovery is designed to prevent unexpected testimony and evidence in the courtroom. During this phase, the attorneys for all parties usually exchange relevant information such as hospital records, clinic charts, laboratory and X-ray tests, and your office medical records.

4. You will be asked to complete a set of interrogatories (written questions) about your education, training, and medical experience. You will also be asked about relevant facts regarding your care of the patient in the case. Your attorney will assist you with your written replies, which are made under oath.

5. Both the deposition of the plaintiff and your deposition will be taken at different times and locations. You will be questioned by the plaintiff's attorney during your deposition. Your attorney will question the plaintiff during his deposition. Other witnesses may or may not be deposed. The deposition is extremely important. Your attorney will prepare you ahead of time.

6. After the depositions, settlement may be negotiated between you, your attorney, the plaintiff, the plaintiff's attorney, and the insurer. To the physician, settlement may be viewed as losing or as admitting negligence or as the least risky and most cost-effective resolution.

7. If neither settlement nor dismissal of the case has occurred, it will go to trial by jury. The plaintiff's case is presented first, then your case. The burden of proof is on the plaintiff. The plaintiff's counsel will have an expert witness testify about the quality of the treatment you rendered to the patient. Your attorney may do the same. You may or may not testify. You will attend the entire trial with your attorney.

8. Alternatively, an arbitration panel will review and evaluate the case, if an arbitration agreement has been signed by both parties before your care of the patient. Usually, this hearing is private, in contrast to a public trial by jury.

9. A verdict is delivered. The jury or arbitration panel will decide if the plaintiff met his burden and the evidence proves you were negligent, and, if negligent, whether your negligence caused injury or death. If this is the case, the jury will decide how much money is to be awarded to the plaintiff.

10. Either side may appeal an adverse verdict, but appeals must be based on questions of law, not on facts. Appeals are heard by a panel of judges, and no new evidence is taken.

YOUR ATTORNEY AND YOU

Although you have the right to consult a personal attorney at your own expense, your malpractice insurance carrier will select and pay the attorney who defends you. Successful malpractice defense attorneys are known to insurers, and you should trust your insurer's judgment to select a capable advocate to defend your case.

A close, professional relationship with your attorney is essential. Just as patients must trust a physician they know little about, you must trust your attorney implicitly. Relate to your attorney just as you want patients to relate to you. Be informative, honest, optimistic, and receptive to professional advice. It is important to talk with your attorney about any previous legal experiences and to avoid enthusiastic agreement with Shakespeare's often-quoted words: "The first thing we do, let's kill all the lawyers." Making your attorney an adversary will only add to your challenges. Instead, devote your energies to educating and assisting him or her.

Once your attorney has been engaged, let her handle all communications, Contact her about legal documents or other communications you receive. Make no personal contact with the plaintiff or anyone involved with the plaintiff. It is unethical for the plaintiff's attorney to communicate with you once you are represented by counsel. Notify your attorney immediately if that happens. Direct all requests from plaintiff's counsel to your attorney. If you are contacted by a plaintiff's attorney *before* you become a defendant (and thus do not have legal counsel), notify your insurance carrier immediately.

THE ROLE OF MEDICAL EXPERTS

Medical experts are essential for medical malpractice lawsuits to go forward and to succeed. The plaintiff must have experts who are willing to testify that your actions fell below medical standards or were unreasonable under the circumstances. Experts are hired by plaintiff's counsel to define the standards of medical care and to testify whether you deviated from those standards and whether your deviation caused the patient's injury. The expert medical witness typically reviews medical records and other materials to make their determinations. They may occasionally examine the patient plaintiff personally.

The plaintiff expert's job is essentially to persuade the jury that, whatever your level of competence, in *this case* you acted negligently and your negligence was a direct cause of injury to the patient. Your attorney may identify experts whose reviews show support for the care or treatment you gave. The defense expert's job is to dispute the plaintiff expert's medical evidence and to support your performance, arguing that it met the standard of care. Experienced malpractice defense attorneys keep a roster of credible experts to call on. Trust that your attorney has weighed many factors (expertise, reputation, availability, juror appeal) when selecting experts. However, your suggestions are likely to be welcomed.

The reactions to the reports of plaintiff's medical experts are fairly predictable. You and your attorney will reject them, argue against their conclusions, and question the expert's qualifications. You may feel guilty because an expert with prestigious credentials disagrees with your care. These are common and normal reactions to criticism. You and your attorney will develop defensive arguments to explain your care of the patient. Identify for your attorney the expert opinions and conclusions you believe can be challenged.

There are some instances of medical negligence for which expert testimony is not needed to establish negligence. Leaving a sponge in a patient's body or operating on the wrong knee are examples of obvious negligence. In such cases, your defense team may admit liability and agree to pay reasonable damages, but even this is not always the case.

Nationally, the tort reform movement has tried many ways to implement meaningful tort reform for medical malpractice. Some ways have been successful, others have not. An area of significant reform has been the regulation of medical expert witnesses. The American Medical Association (AMA) has implemented a specific policy with guidelines that can be used to determine the credibility of a medical expert in malpractice cases. In 2004, the AMA adopted an affirmation statement for all medical experts to sign before taking a case [65]. The statement reads as follows:

American Medical Association
Expert Witness Affirmation Statement

I affirm that I will adhere to the following principles guiding expert witness testimony:

1. Physicians have an ethical obligation to assist in the administration of justice.
2. Physicians are legally and ethically obligated to tell the truth.
3. Subject to the rules of court, physicians, when testifying as expert witnesses in cases alleging medical negligence, should

   ▪ Review the medical information in the case and testify fairly to its content;
   ▪ Review the standards of practice prevailing at the time of the occurrence;
   ▪ Indicate when their beliefs may differ from standards of practice prevailing at the time of the occurrence or when their beliefs differ from generally accepted theories of medical science;
   ▪ Testify impartially and objectively and not adopt a position of advocacy except as spokesmen for the field of special knowledge they represent;
   ▪ Testify only in matters in which they have relevant clinical experience or academic knowledge;
   ▪ Be prepared to distinguish between actual negligence and an unfortunate medical outcome; and
   ▪ Be prepared to state the bases of their opinions.

4. Compensation for expert testimony of physicians should be reasonable and commensurate with the time and effort required of them. It is unethical for a physician to accept compensation that is contingent upon the outcome of litigation.
5. Physicians, when testifying as medical experts, are engaged in the practice of medicine.
6. Physicians should accept and facilitate the peer review of medical expert testimony.
   Date: _____
   Name: _____

Reprinted with kind permission from the American Medical Association.

Many state medical societies have adopted ethical guidelines for medical experts and disciplinary procedures to be used when the guidelines are violated. It appears these guidelines may be having some effect based on the number of referrals for expert witnesses. If the expert purposely shades his opinion to support the attorney paying him, justice is not served. The AMA should be applauded for taking such a significant step to advance tort reform. It is encouraging that our national and local medical societies are getting more involved in a meaningful way to better represent physicians. Our societies have had their heads in the sand far too long. Nevertheless, most medical experts are honest physicians who give honest objective opinions of the cases they review. There are a few, however, who have abused their position, causing needless trauma for the legal process and the defendant physician. National regulation has been long overdue.

11

The Pocket Guide

When one is not familiar with all the detailed steps to navigating the litigation process, it is helpful to have a guide. Angela Dodge, a psychologist who specializes in medical malpractice defense, has developed a pocket guide for physicians [66]. She notes it is similar to the "Cliff Notes" some students use in college when they lack the time or motivation to read the entire text. The pocket guide is an organized list of summaries, condensed points, tips, and avoidable traps doctors can use as a quick reference resource. With Dr. Dodge's permission, the pocket guide is as follows.

THINGS TO REMEMBER ABOUT MALPRACTICE LAWSUITS

The key determination in any malpractice lawsuit is whether your care fell below the "standard of care" for your specialty.

1. The plaintiff must prove his case by a "preponderance of the evidence" and must use medical experts to do so.
2. Yours is a civil case to determine liability and damages, not guilt or punishment.
3. Lawsuits are filed against even the best doctors and have little to do with your track record.
4. Most malpractice lawsuits are dropped or settled before trial; many are won at trial.
5. Lawsuits are won through team defense efforts; you are an important team member whose active participation is critical to success.

THINGS TO REMEMBER ABOUT EMOTIONAL REACTIONS

1. Common reactions include annoyance, diminished confidence, self-criticism, overanalysis, resentment, anger, fear, anxiety, and worry about loss of control, disbelief, and denial.
2. Expect to be on an emotional roller-coaster to some extent.
3. Being proactive and cooperating in your defense will help you regain some sense of control.
4. Positive self-talk and imaging will help reduce anxiety and have a calming effect.
5. It is intelligent, not weak, to rely on family and friends for emotional support.

THINGS TO REMEMBER ABOUT DEPOSITIONS

1. Depositions are taken to assist the *opposing party* and are of no benefit to you. A deposition is not the place to tell your story. Do not try to persuade opposing counsel that the plaintiff's case is weak.
2. Depositions result in a typed transcript that will be thoroughly scrutinized by opposing counsel in the hopes of discovering damaging admissions, inconsistencies, falsehoods, or other facts not previously known to him.
3. Depositions are not conversations, and none of the principles of polite social conversation apply. Just the opposite is true: question and answer exchanges proceed with completely different rules.
4. Opposing counsel's goals are to cast a wide net to gather information, evaluate your strength as a witness, and test her case themes.
5. Preparation for a deposition with your attorney is essential to your performance, and you should insist on it.

THINGS TO REMEMBER ABOUT YOUR GOALS AT DEPOSITION

1. Tell the truth and do not guess.
2. Listen actively and carefully to every word in every question.

3. Be succinct, accurate, and precise in your answers.
4. Take your time and do not try too hard.
5. Keep your cool no matter how much tempers heat up.

THINGS TO REMEMBER ABOUT LISTENING

1. Everyday listening is different from the kind of active listening required at a deposition or trial.
2. Barriers to active listening include "out-listening" (listening only long enough to surmise what is being said), "selective listening" (hearing only what you want to), and "challenge listening" (focusing on your anticipated response rather than to what is being said). These barriers can prevent you from properly diagnosing and responding to questions under cross-examination.
3. Active listening is your most powerful weapon against opposing counsel. It protects you from being intimidated or trapped.
4. By listening carefully you can avoid common mistakes, such as jumping ahead to questions you anticipate, answering too quickly, improving upon weak questions, or becoming distracted.
5. Use your diagnostic skills to determine what kind of question you are being asked and clarify any misunderstandings before answering. Ask for clarification if the question is leading, ambiguous, hypothetical, or intended to be provocative.
6. Listen for "mental alarms" such as inflammatory words, mischaracterizations or misstatements, embedded assumptions, negative words, absolutes, double negatives, or ambiguous phrases.
7. Practice active listening by visualizing spoken words, paraphrasing, and correcting social speech.

THINGS TO REMEMBER ABOUT ANSWERING QUESTIONS

1. The most common errors are volunteering information, failing to listen carefully, and losing emotional composure. Most errors result from lack of understanding of the purposes and goals of the deposition.

2. The most common fears are that one's testimony will be manipulated or that opposing counsel will badger a witness into saying something unintended.
3. Many doctors fear memory failures, but there is no need to be overly concerned about this. In addition to your unassisted recall, you can rely on memory refreshers, records and lab results, and your professional routines.
4. Certain areas of questioning can be expected to be covered at your deposition. As it is taken during the "discovery" phase, expect a wide range of questions, some of which may appear to you irrelevant.
5. There are certain rules you should follow in giving a deposition. The most important are to tell the truth at all times. Listen carefully to every word in every question, keep your answers brief, and make certain you understand a question completely before answering, stay within your realm of expertise, use positive action words to talk about what you did, and maintain a professional demeanor.
6. Because attorneys are professional questioners, they are skilled at maneuvering you into certain response modes. You can avoid these tricks and traps if you are aware of them. Some common traps are putting words in your mouth, inviting you to volunteer information, cutting short your answers, jumping from topic to topic, pointing out inconsistencies, asking the same question in different forms, focusing on failures and inducing guilt, exaggerating the importance of inconsequential facts, and catching you off guard by dropping "bombshells."
7. While giving testimony, avoid negative words, medical jargon, hesitant language, and deferential titles such as "sir" and "madam."

THINGS TO REMEMBER ABOUT GOING TO TRIAL

1. It is unlikely your case will go to trial, but you should always be prepared to do so.
2. Your testimony at trial will be different than at deposition because this is now the time to tell your story.
3. At trial, view your role as one of educator, not defendant.

4. You will be subjected to direct examination by your attorney and cross-examination by opposing counsel. Listen intently, diagnose questions, seek clarification, and answer questions carefully, regardless of who is asking them.

5. Jurors will be evaluating not only what you say, but how you say it. Your demeanor on the witness stand should reflect the three Cs: Competence, Confidence, and Compassion. You must win the esteem and respect of jurors if you hope to persuade them with your testimony.

6. You are being assessed by jurors at all times, so watch those nervous tics and annoying habits. Always be completely professional in the courtroom.

7. Pretrial jitters are expected and can be reduced by familiarizing yourself with the courtroom before the trial, using imagery and positive affirmations, and using relaxation techniques. Some period of "decompression" may be needed after the trial is completed.

When good doctors get sued: a practical guide for physicians involved in malpractice lawsuits, 2001 Angela M. Dodge: reprinted with kind permission from Dodge & Associates.

12

The Litigation Stress Syndrome

Anybody can sue anyone for any reason at any time.

The most significant problem with malpractice litigation is the high personal toll it takes on the physician, his family, staff, and oftentimes his other patients. For doctors to do what they do, it is necessary for us to have a strong sense of self, a firm confidence that we know what is best for the patient and that we will make things better for the patient at all times. I am reminded of this whenever I am explaining to a young couple in the middle of the night in the emergency room why it is necessary for me to take their 6-year-old only child to surgery for an emergency appendectomy. The difficulty with this premise is it assumes we posses a degree of control over the patient disease and circumstances that we do not have. It also assumes a level of infallibility that we do not have.

What in effect happens during a malpractice suit is we physicians many times suffer a major loss. It is a loss of the illusion that, because we are well-trained, intelligent, and committed doctors, we will not make mistakes and can control life-threatening situations if we work hard. It is a loss of the illusion that because we are good doctors, kind and gentle, all our patients will love us and would not dare sue us. We understand intellectually, of course, that a certain percentage of physicians will be sued, but emotionally we do not believe that will happen to us if we always do the right thing. Actually, whether we are sued or not in our practice lifetime has little to do with us and much to do with what the patient thinks, their advisors, and their circumstance. Indeed, anybody can sue anyone for any reason at any time [21].

We are sometimes victims of our own good doctor syndrome. This is the syndrome that makes us feel guilty if we take a vacation longer than 2 weeks or if we even take a vacation at all! It makes us feel guilty if we turn off our cell phone or beeper when we go out to dinner or the movies, although we may have no sick patients in the hospital or we have a qualified trusted colleague covering our practice for us at the time. All these issues can contribute to a significant amount of grief when involved with malpractice litigation. Additionally, malpractice attorneys usually follow the motto "throw it up against the wall and see what sticks." When they send you a letter or a complaint, it will allege that you did many dangerous things, not just one. This confrontational approach is designed to put pressure on you and add to your grief, allowing them to extort a larger settlement or money damage amount.

Dr. Kenneth Olsen, a psychiatrist at Bridges Psychiatric Services, notes that physicians may experience "complicated grief, which disallows effective resolution of the suit or loss, may include: unbidden memories or intrusive fantasies; strong pangs of severe emotion; feelings of loneliness or emptiness; avoidance of reminders of the loss; sleep interference; and loss of interest in work or recreational activities" [59]. Dr. Olsen further notes that "the impact of malpractice litigation on the physician is insidious, often overwhelming and difficult to process. Physicians are accustomed to being in control and invulnerable."

Dr. Charles, a psychiatrist, observes that some patient adverse events may result in traumatic life events for the physician. She relates "In most circumstances, physicians feel closely related to their patients...A traumatic event is not a discrete event that is over and done with immediately. It generally triggers a process that inflicts other losses to which we must adapt. A recent widow not only lost her husband but also experiences changes in her social and financial status. For those of us in healthcare, a traumatic event may generate the additional trauma of legal action with its threat of serious personal, financial, and professional losses."

To provide a stronger and more stable mental foundation, there are a number of things we can do to treat the good doctor syndrome. Some actions are to develop our support network, talk to our family and close friends, put the lawsuit in perspective, learn more about the litigation process (such as reading this book), do more fun things, and listen more to our spouse.

13

Perspective: When the Physician Becomes a Patient

It was a beautiful May evening in 1999. Lorena and I were having a terrific dinner with friends at Walt and Patsy's house in Glendora. We were all laughing about different things. During the evening, one of the guests mentioned he needed to make an appointment to see his proctologist. Much joking followed. I remember thinking to myself that I was still having problems with those hemorrhoids and should probably get them checked. I whispered this into my wife's ear. She agreed and suggested that I do it as soon as possible.

Tuesday of the following week, I called my good friend Dr. Ranga Panguluri, a gastroenterologist. I told him I wanted a colonoscopy. He said, "Sure, Bill, no problem. When do you want to have it done?" I told him this week. He said he was going to Chicago on Thursday but could do it that morning before he left. He called me back to say he had set it up for 8:30 A.M. on Thursday at Inter-Community Hospital's GI Laboratory. I asked how long the procedure would take because I had to give a lecture at Northridge Community Hospital on medical malpractice. He told me the procedure takes about 10–15 minutes and thus should have no effect on my noon lecture. I said okay.

After taking my oral Fleets phosfasoda prep the night before, I met Ranga at 8:30 on Thursday morning. I remember being struck with how modern and high tech the GI Lab looked. As a practicing general surgeon, I have done sigmoid examinations for years in my office but without the fancy monitors and TV screens. The nurse was very nice and helpful. Ranga, the nurse, and I were all in a very relaxed mood as the exam started. We were laughing and making small talk. I could simultaneously see what Ranga was seeing by watching the TV monitor. Within 30 seconds into the exam, Ranga said, "Oh my God, Bill, do you see that?" I quietly said, "Yes, I do." As a general surgeon myself, I have seen hundreds of these lesions in my patients over the years. It was an infiltrating adenocarcinoma that took up almost one-half of the bowel lumen, located at about 10 cm.

Time stopped for me instantly! The room suddenly became very quiet. Ranga felt horrible. He kept apologizing to me as if it were his fault. He completed the examination and gave me some other technical information. They asked me if I wanted them to call Lorena, whose office was just down the hall; she worked at Intercommunity Hospital in management as Director of Medical Staff Services. He offered to tell her for me. I said no, that I would tell her myself. I dressed and slowly walked to Lorena's office.

My approach with patients is to always tell bad news within the first couple of sentences. I told Lorena, after closing the door, that it was cancerous. She embraced me and we shared an emotional moment. Soon afterward, Ranga arrived. He again apologized and the three of us shared another emotional moment. Ranga then left for his flight to Chicago, and I drove to Northridge to give my lecture.

THE PLAN

Having treated this problem in others, I knew major surgery was a requirement. I called my colleague (and one of my best friends), Dr. Tim Ching. Tim and I have worked together in surgery for more than 15 years. He is hard working, intelligent, honest, and an excellent surgeon. I told him what I had and that I wanted him to do my surgery. There was a pause in our conversation and then he said, "I could do that, but to be honest with you, I don't think that is the best way to go." He went on to explain that he regularly works with Dr. Luis Martinez, one of the colon surgery specialists. The colon specialists do a different type of procedure that he feels is better than what we general surgeons do. I followed Tim's advice and met with Dr. Martinez. He was very confident and thorough, two qualities I like in a surgeon. I spoke to my longtime friend and family physician, Dr. Dale Kellon.

He expressed profound sorrow. Dale agreed to coordinate all the paperwork with Lorena to make sure I got all the care I needed. I spoke to Dr. Jonathan Tye, my cardiologist. He treats me for hypertension. I had a routine EKG and treadmill a few months earlier that were completely normal. I asked John to be around on the day of surgery. He assured me he would. The next issue was whether to have radiation preoperatively or postoperatively. I called Dr. Au, the radiotherapist, and he opined that I should definitely have it. All the physicians agreed that it should be pre-op. I was very leery of radiation therapy. I knew it not only killed the tumor cells but also damaged normal tissue. Nevertheless, I agreed that the benefit was worth the risk.

WHO TO TELL AND WHEN

Deciding who to tell and when was difficult. Other than the physicians involved, no one knew but Lorena and I. We told the kids (who are all adult now) on the telephone, and then we invited each of them to come for a family weekend in Mexico after one of our monthly clinic trips. We had a terrific weekend with the kids in Baja, and not once was my illness mentioned… it was not necessary. My initial inclination was that no one else should know. I knew that was impossible because I had decided to be treated at the hospital where Lorena and I both work. I knew I had to tell the "Magnificent Seven" surgery group (Surgical Care Associates, Inc). This is a group of six other surgeons with whom I had worked and served as president for more than 8 years. They were also some of my closest physician friends, and Dr. Tim Ching was a part of the group. I decided to tell them simultaneously, at the end of one of our monthly meetings. Telling them was much more difficult than I ever imagined. As I began to tell them about my problems, I was having difficulty emotionally finding the right words. Tim spoke and completed giving the group the information. The other five members of the group were stunned. As all were surgeons themselves, they immediately started asking clinical questions for more details about the tumor and my treatment plan. I patiently and slowly answered each of their questions. Each of them said their prayers would be with me and that they would be around on the day of surgery. Drs. Yeo and Daluvoy said it would be okay. Drs. Hameed and Baron gave me a hug. Drs. Tim Ching and Edillon walked me to my car to talk more. As I was driving away, I remembered feeling some relief that I had finally told them but also being surprised at how difficult it was for me to talk about it with my colleagues and some of my closest friends. I wanted to tell other friends, such as Patsy and Armando, but I could not. It was just too difficult.

Now my surgery date had been set, the preoperative radiotherapy was proceeding, and Drs. Au and Sevilla were very helpful. However, I needed to choose an anesthesiologist. One name came to my mind, Ben Shwachman. I have known Ben for almost 20 years. At times we have been on different sides of various political issues at the hospital, but he is a good person and an excellent anesthesiologist. Also, Ben is a practicing attorney. When I was getting my law degree, Ben was very helpful as a friend and mentor with whom I could talk. I caught Ben one day between cases and we went to a small office close to the surgery area where we could speak privately. I explained to him about my problem and told him I wanted him to be my anesthesiologist. "Absolutely", he said. Again, it was an emotionally difficult conversation for me. He was very encouraging; he shared some personal experiences and told me not to worry. He gave me a hug and we left. Now I felt that I had done all that I could do to prepare for surgery. I have never been in the hospital as patient in the 51 years of my life. I was not afraid of surgery, I was *terrified* of surgery! In the 25 years since I graduated from Yale, I had seen a lot of surgery, and I knew all the things that could go wrong.

SURGERY DAY

Dwight, our oldest son, had come over Sunday night to stay and go with us on Monday. My surgery was scheduled for 7:30 A.M. Monday morning. I liked the early morning time because I felt the surgery team would be fresh. Dwight, Lorena, and I arrived at the hospital at about 6 A.M. I wore my surgical scrubs from home. As we got on the elevator to go up to surgery, Dr. Calvin Schneider joined us on the elevator. He wished me well and said he would pray for me. In the outpatient holding area, I changed clothes and was assigned my bed to wait for my 7:30 surgery. Lorena and Dwight waited with me. Everyone was very nice to us. A number of the surgery nurses and transport staff came by to say hi and to wish me well. I was trying desperately to control my emotions but it was almost impossible at this point. Ben came in to listen to my heart and lungs and to see if I had any questions about the anesthesia. I told him no, and he said he would see me inside.

Then Harold arrived; it was 7:30 A.M. Harold is the main surgical technician and transporter at the hospital. He said, "Doctor, it's time to go." I said okay and kissed Lorena and Dwight goodbye. I have worked with Harold and the surgery nurses and staff since 1981 when I first joined the medical staff. This same surgery staff has helped me take care of hundreds of patients and now they were taking care of me. As Harold rolled me down the hall to my operating room, the surgical nurses and technicians lined both sides of the hallway; each physically touched me as I went by, and they all wished me well. Then I arrived at operating room #4. They took me in and the room seemed very bright. Nuca, one of the nurses and a Walnut resident, welcomed me to the room and told me everything would be okay. She had them to turn the music on and asked me if I liked the selection. I said it was fine. The surgical staff knew I like to operate with soft music when I am the surgeon so they assumed I would like the same when I was the surgical patient. They were right. The music was very relaxing and soothing. Ben and Dr. Ruben Martinez, a fellow anesthesiologist, started my two IVs. I kept telling myself I wanted to go to sleep quickly. I routinely stand at the bedside and hold the hand of my patients as they go to sleep. Nuca and Linda both now stood at my bedside and held my hand as I went to sleep.

The surgery was supposed to take 3 hours but it actually took 6.5 hours! The surgical nurses had set an hourly relay to let Lorena know how things were going in surgery. She was very worried because of the prolonged time. When the surgery was over, I was both in excruciating pain and confused. Jenny, the OR supervisor, allowed Lorena at her request to come in and see me in the recovery room This small act of kindness was extremely important. Lorena was able to see that I was okay. I do not remember anything in the recovery room but seeing Lorena. Once I saw her I calmed down because I knew I was alive and my guardian angel was there watching over me. She slept in the hospital at my bedside every night taking care of me with the nurses. During my 5-day stay in the hospital, many good people visited, called, sent gifts, and prayed. I was discharged on my fourth postoperative day. I am now back at work full time caring for my patients. By the way, the tumor was completely removed, I did not need a colostomy, and all the lymph nodes were negative. God has smiled on me yet again and given me another chance.

It is imperative we physicians keep a proper perspective as we deal with the various changes in healthcare. We must prioritize and remember what is most important. Our faith, family, and friends help to remind us that no matter what circumstances we are experiencing, the glass is always half full. We need to spend more time nourishing these positive elements that strengthen us.

Therefore, as we arm ourselves with knowledge that allows us to provide good patient care, while simultaneously fighting legal and political battles, may we always remember that life really is too short not to enjoy it. We are privileged to be a part of the greatest profession in the world. We are physicians!

14
Summary

Medical malpractice is negligence. A plaintiff must prove the physician had a duty of care and breached that duty. Also, it must be proven the breach actually caused damages to the patient and that the patient was damaged. Careful documentation is an effective shield against some needless litigation. Only the physician can give informed consent. The consent must include risks, benefits, and alternative treatments. Required culturally competent care is a reality. Respect transcends all cultures and is also an effective shield to needless litigation.

Disruptive physician behavior is a national healthcare problem that is rapidly growing. Not only are there more episodes of aberrant physician behavior, the definition of what is unacceptable doctor conduct is now broader. Society in general and hospital organizations in particular are less willing to tolerate this behavior since national standards have been developed. These standards suggest that disruptive behavior impacts not only patient care but also patient safety. Appropriate pain management is extremely important and may help the surgeon avoid liability that is not covered by medical malpractice insurance.

Finally, a truism: "anybody can sue anybody for any reason at any time." Knowledge of the law and changing medical legal regulations will not completely insulate surgeons from all malpractice litigation and medical legal concerns. However, this knowledge will decrease needless litigation, mitigate financial damage for the physician, and restore physician empowerment. Life is but a journey to be enjoyed passionately and enthusiastically. Faith, family, and friends are vital for a happy perspective.

References

1. Szalados J. Understanding malpractice: the law of medical negligence. General Surgery News 2006;33:24–30.
2. Malpractice: patients asked to help. Surgical Rounds, June 2005, p. 293.
3. Choctaw W. The Trauma Surgeon in Harm's Way: Medical Legal Implications. Presented at 11th Annual Trauma Critical Care Symposium: New Frontiers in Trauma Care, Pasadena, CA, 2004.
4. Tort reform: the truth of the matter. AM News, 2006, p. 25.
5. To Err Is Human: Building a Safer Health System. Institute of Medicine, 1999. www.iom.edu.
6. Becker C. Pa releases infection data. Modern Healthcare, July 2005, p. 16.
7. Stone G. Constitutional Law. Boston: Little Brown, 1996:IXI–IXXVI.
8. Fletcher G. Basic Concepts of Legal Thought. Oxford: Oxford University Press, 1996.
9. Wisconsin court strikes liability care. AM News 2005;48:29.
10. Raske K. End the stalemate on tort reform. Modern Healthcare, August 2005, p. 34.
11. Dr. David. Issues & Allegations: Medical Malpractice. www.americanvoice2004.org/health/malpractice.html.
12. National Practitioner Data Bank. 2007. www. npdb-hipdb.hrsa.gov.
13. Sorrel A. Courts set limits on confidentiality. AM News, February 2006, p. 59.
14. Nolan J. Black's Law Dictionary. St. Paul: West Publishing, 1990.
15. Furrow B. Health Law, 3rd ed. St. Paul: West Publishing, 1997.
16. Definition of Koch's Postulates. www.medterms.com.
17. Camazine B. Pitfalls of appendicitis. Contemp Surg 2005;6:199–201.
18. Alberts T. Know bylaws that protect medical staff. AMNews.com, July 2005.
19. Olson K. Recognizing the symptoms of malpractice stress syndrome. Psychiatric Times 2000;17:1–4.
20. Baker T. The Medical Malpractice Myth. Chicago: University of Chicago Press, 2005.
21. Studdert D. Claims errors and compensation payments in medical malpractice litigation. N Engl J Med 2006;355:734–735.
22. Kodner T, Spiegler M, Freeman D, Choctaw W. Ethical and Legal Considerations. New York: Springer, 2007:735–763.
23. Cotton P. Analysis of 59 ERCP lawsuits: mainly about indications. Gastrointest Endosc 2006;63:1–7.
24. Greene F. Using science to battle litigation risk. General Surgery News, February 2007, p. 3.
25. Frangou C. The science of litigation. General Surgery News 2007;34:10–12.

26. Risk Management Malpractice. PowerPoint presentation, CAP-MPT, Los Angeles, CA, 2000.

27. Identifying legal landmines. Southern California Physician, November 2006, p. 45.

28. Tom P. Illegible Handwriting Can Contribute to Medical Errors. MBC Action Report, 2005, p. 12.

29. Johnson L. Right way to correct a record. Medical Economics, June 2005, p. 37.

30. JCAHO 2007 NPSG PowerPoint Presentation. www.JCAHO.com., 2007.

31. Frangou C. Can you fire a patient? General Surgery News 2006;33:1.

32. Gilliland J. Patient Abandonment. Gilliland Markette and Milligan, LLP. www.gilliland.com.

33. Federal Patient Self Determination Act 42 U.S.C. 1395. Federal Register 1990;60:123.

34. Adams D. Patients list 7 key traits of good doctors. American Medical News, April 2006, p. 12.

35. Principles of consent. Risk Management News, Citrus Valley Health Partners, 2000.

36. Arbitration news: the revised arbitration agreement. CAP-MPT Bulletin, August, 2006.

37. Weiss G. Malpractice Mess: Is This the Way Out? Medical Economics, 2004. www.memag.com.

38. Office of Minority Health. A Practical Guide for Implementing the Recommended National Standards for CLAS in Health Care. December 2001. www.omhrc.gov/clas.

39. New Jersey: Cultural Competency Training 2005. www.cmwf.org.

40. O'Reilly K. Data highlight health gaps for Hispanic kids. American Medical News, September 2005, p. 13.

41. Silver J. Movie Day at the Supreme Court. I Know It When I See It. www.library.findlaw.com.

42. American Medical Association (AMA) Policy: H-140.918 Disruptive Physician. www.ama-assn.org.

43. Report of Special Committee on Professional Conduct & Ethics. Federation of State Medical Boards of the United States, Inc., Dallas, TX.

44. Choctaw W. Disruptive Physician Behavior. PowerPoint presentation, 2007. Available from the author.

45. Salas. AB 632 (Whistleblower) section 1278.5, CA Health and Safety Code, October 14, 2007.

46. Springer H. Another whistle blower loses again. Medical Staff Leader, September 2005, pp. 1–3.

47. Huntoon L. Sham peer review and the courts. J Am Physicians Surg 2006;11:4–5.

48. Grounds for Medical Board Discipline. California Medical Association, 2004. www.camnet.org.

49. Schecter W. Preoperative pain management. General Surgery News, June 2005.

50. National Pain Forum Symposium, Pfizer, San Diego, CA, October 2005.

51. Ayazi K. Elder abuse claims: what doctors need to know. Capsules. A Risk Management Publication, CAP, Inc., 4th Quarter, 2005.

52. King S. JCHHO Pain Standards. Geriatric Times, November/December 2000, 1(4).

53. Caveney B. The promises of E-health: why are doctors so reluctant to adopt some new technologies. MD Consult–Student Union Story, 2007, pp. 1–5.

54. Wendling P. EMR errors skew data on quality. American Medical News, March 2006, p. 16.

55. Norbut M. Agent for change. American Medical News, April 2006, p. 14.

56. Adams D. Most doctors slow to integrate quality data into their practices. American Medical News, June 6, 2005.

57. Terry N. Cyber-malpractice: legal exposure for cyber-medicine. Am J Law Med 1999;25:327–366.

58. Doctors are beginning to accept E-alerts: study. Modern Healthcare, February 2006, p. 32.

59. Olsen K. Recognizing the symptoms of malpractice stress syndrome. Psychiatric Times, April 2000;17(4).

60. Responding to unanticipated outcomes in patient care. www.smanot. org, January 2006, pp. 1–16.

61. Kaufan D. Healing Words: The Power of I'm Sorry in Medical Practice. MDConsult.com, 2007, pp. 1–4.

62. Doctors want the option to apologize to patients. American Medical News, April 2006, p. 12.

63. Mattow A. Disclosure of medical errors. Pediatr Clin N Am 2006;53:1–10.

64. Charles S. Adverse Events Stress and Litigation. Oxford: Oxford University Press, 2005.

65. Expert Witness Guidelines. www.cmanet.org, January 2006.

66. Dodge A. When Good Doctors Get Sued. Olalla, WA: BookPartners Incorporated, 2001.

Further Reading

ACS responds to pay for performance proposals: quality measures should be clinically valid, widely accepted, feasible, and inexpensive. Surgery News, August 2006, p. 14.

Adams D. Appeals of disciplinary actions could become more open. American Medical News, September 2005, pp. 14–19.

Adams D. Doctor's self insurance found to meet standard. AM News, 2005.

Adams D. Practice pressures diminish care. American Medical News, April 2006, p. 15.

AMA adds Tennessee to malpractice crisis list. Modern Healthcare, 2006, p. 3.

Amatayakul M. Managing individual rights requirement under HIPAA privacy. American Health Information Management Association, June 2001, pp. 16–64.

AM News Staff. Georgia court rules venue provision in tort reform law unconstitutional. American Medical News, March 2006, p. 8.

AM News Staff. Another state added to liability crisis list. American Medical News, March 2006, p. 11.

AM News Staff. 21 reasons why we need tort reform now. American Medical News, March 2006, p. 24.

Average indemnity payment per cardiovascular or thoracic surgeon involved in malpractice case. Surgical News, 2006.

Barr P. Lingering side effects: DRG changes called positive but other woes remain. Modern Healthcare, August 2006, p. 17.

Becker C. Ban has fiscal repercussions. Modern Healthcare, March 2006, p. 17.

Benko L. Medical rates are flat: study. American Medical News, March 2006, p. 31.

Bullet Proofing Your Medical Practice: Risk Management Techniques for Physicians That Work. www.seak.com/bookRMtqc.htm.

Burda D. Improving on improvement. Modern Healthcare, March 2006, p. 18.

Caveney B. The promises of E-health: why are doctors so reluctant to adopt some new technologies. MD Consult, 2007, pp. 1–5.

Checking Your Physician Profile on Medical Board of California Web Site: Public Disclosure of Malpractice Settlements. MBC Action Report, 2005, p. 8.

Chin T. Bill seeks to assist doctors in buying health technology. American Medical News, April 2006, p. 14.

Chin T. Man sues insurer for not paying hospital stay. American Medical News, July 2005, p. 23.

Choctaw W. Medico-legal challenges of the difficult patient. Presentation, March 2004.

Chritman K. Hospital overcharging. J Am Physicians Surg 2006;11:6.

Clinical guidelines often penned by industry bedfellows. General Surgery News, February 2006, p. 13.

Conn J. Big in Rhode Island. Modern Healthcare, March 2006, p. 30.

Cossman D. JCAHO unplugged. General Surgery News 2005;32:1.

Cossman D. The death of open surgery. General Surgery News 2006;33:1.

Covey M. Are you practicing medicine outside of California (do you really know)? Bulletin CAP-MPT, January 2006.

Croasdale M. Call for stricter CME gift rules get mixed reviews. American Medical News, 2006, p. 19.

Dahl D. Schiavo case demonstrates need for clarity. Surgery News, June 2005, p. 6.

Doi A. Medical school enactment hits record. Modern Healthcare, October 2005, p. 32.

Donnelly T. Malpractice risk management: lessons in patient safety. Contemp Surg 2006;62(9):425.

Dougherty C. A surgical action for surgeon with endoscopy induced injury. General Surgery News, February 2006.

Electronic record-keeping. Surgical Rounds, June 2005, p. 265.

Eliminating Healthcare Disparities: You Can Make a Difference. AMNews.com, September 27, 2006.

Elliot V. Experts: Cox 2's still have role in pain care. American Medical News, April 2006, p. 46.

Evans M. AHH blasts staffing standards. Modern Healthcare, March 2006, p. 10.

Evans M. Compensating nurses. Modern Healthcare, July 2005, p. 12.

Evans M. Health education cuts sting. Modern Healthcare, 2006, p. 30.

Evidence-Based Tips Help Hospital Prevent Patient Safety. 2006. www.MDconsult.com.

Federal Patient Self Determination Act 42 U.S.C. 1395.

Fong T. Medicaid limits: HHS proposes restricting federal funds to cost of care. Modern Healthcare, August 2006.

Fong T. More dollars for doctors. Modern Healthcare, July 2005, p. 12.

Foster J. Changes in Malpractice Lawsuits. February 2003. www.whiteandWilliams.com.

Frangou C. Another day, another dollar lost working as a general surgeon. General Surgery News 2006;33:1.

Frei R. Trauma surgeons voice wish to broaden the practice. General Surgery News, February 2006, p. 15.

Frieden G. Heart surgery patient awarded $5 million in fraud case. Elsevier Global Med News, Surgical News, 2006.

Frieden J. New hospital database from Medicare expands information access to doctors and patients alike. Surgery News, June 2005, p. 5.

Full-court press on malpractice. Surgical Rounds, June 2005, p. 294.

General surgery still largely dominated by men. Surgical News 2006;12:2.

Ginion L. Language becoming an issue for health insurers. Los Angeles Times, March 20, 2006, p.c1.

Glendinning D. Delegate set strict standard in pay for performance program. American Medical News 2005;48:1–4.

Glendining D. Medicare reimbursement frozen; focus returns to pay for performance. AMA News 2006;49:7.

Gonzalez D. New Study: Tort Reforms Reduce Medical Malpractice Premiums. www.thepiaq.org., 2006.

Green F. Safety in the OR; let's talk! General Surgery News, January 2006, p. 3.

Groszy D. Patient Safety & Quality Improvement Act of 2005. Capsules. A Risk Management Publication, CAP, Inc., 4th Quarter, 2005.

Harris S. Payers won't pay. Know your contract remedies. American Medical News, September 2005, p. 18.

Health disparities experienced by Hispanics: United States. JAMA 2004;292:19.

HHMC calls for ban on gifts to physicians. Modern Healthcare, February 2006.

Howe R. Radical change: time to discard the routine, medical tort liability system! The Leading Edge 2004;20(3). www.acpe.org/leadingedge.

JCAHO to Conduct Unannounced Resurveys in All Accreditation Program in 2006. The Joint Commission Perspective 2003;23(5):6.

Johnston W. Medical opinion under siege. General Surgery News 2005;32:1.

Johnston W. Witnessing justice. General Surgery News 2006;33:1.

Jury Awards $5.6 Million in Screwdriver Case. www.msnbc.msn.com, 2006.

Kaplan M. Front page news. Modern Healthcare, November 2005, p. 22.

Kaufman D. Apologizing & Offering Fair Compensation Can Circumvent Malpractice Suits. www.MDconsult.com, 2005.

Leeson P. Implementing the 2007 Medical Staff Performance Improvement Standards. IMQ Essentials for MS Leader Seminar, San Francisco, CA, April 2007.

Lenckus D. Attentive docs minimize lawsuits. Modern Healthcare, December 12, 2005, p. 39.

Malpractice Cases Go Unreported to Data Bank. AMNews.com, 11/7/2005, p. 22.

Managed Care Trends. AMNews.com, 2005.

Mantone A. Tenet settle cases. Modern Healthcare, August 2006, p. 18.

Mechcatie E. Medication Error Rates Are Highest in Perioperative Area in American Hospitals. Elsevier Global Medical News, 2007. www.MDconsult.com.

Median compensatory Tony awards leveled off in malpractice cases. Surgery News, August 2005.

Medical staff doctors behavior policy. Medical Staff Advocate CME, October 2005, p. 4.

Michigan paying doctors to track outcome. General Surgery News, January 2006.

Miller C. Fixing the record after the fact. Don't even be tempted. Capsules. A Risk Management Publication, CAP, Inc., 1st Quarter, 2006.

Miller C. Fixing the Record After the Fact: Don't Even Be Tempted. Capsules CAP-MPT, January/February 2006.

Monesmith E. Managing pain after total joint replacement. Orthop Technol Rev 2006;8:1–6.

New device teaches surgeons a kinder, gentler touch. General Surgery News, February 2006, p. 18.

Norbut M. Doctors ask court to compel Cigna to pay. American Medical News, September 2005, p. 13.

Noumayor L, Bendavid R, Duh Q, et al. Managing unique needs in inguinal hernia repair. Contemp Surg 2005;61:384–389.

On-call physicians "no show" liability. American Medical Association Legal Advisor, January 2000, pp. 1–4.

O'Reilly K. Only 1 medical school uses classic version of Hippocratic Oath. AM News, February 2006, p. 9.

Ownby G. It's always better to be prepared not just lucky. Bulletin CAP-MPT, 2006.

Pain After Surgery. www.emedicinehealth.com/articles, 2005.

Pain Control After Surgery: Pain Medication. Family.doctor.org/259.sm/, 2005.

Physicians Right to Access Peer Review Records. Legal Advisor, American Medical Association, January 2000, pp. 2–3.

Report of Special Committee on Professional Conduct & Ethics. Federation of State Medical Boards of the United States, Inc., Dallas, TX.

Researchers put forth quality indicators for geriatrics surgery. General Surgery News 2006;33:1.

Reynolds N. Investigating Physician Suspected of Suffering from a Disabling Mental and Physical Condition That Poses a Threat to Patient Care. MBC Action Report, 2005, p. 6.

Robeznieks A. Immune to marketing? Modern Healthcare, September 2005, p. 52.

Robeznieks A. Medical records most meet health-record criteria. Modern Healthcare, September 2005, p. 52.

Robeznieks A. Support seen for Oregon law. Modern Healthcare, October 2005, p. 32.

Robeznieks A. 100K lives falling short. Modern Healthcare, March 2006, p. 12.

Romano M. Combining doc data. American Medical News, March 2006, p. 7.

Romano M. Holding steady. Modern Healthcare, July 2005, pp. 1–5.

Romano M. Malpractice not the issue. Modern Healthcare, July 2005, p. 8.

Romeno M. AMH D—specialty docs. Modern Healthcare, February 2006, p. 7.

Shore E. If a Colleague Is Careless. Medical Economics, 2006. www.memag.com.

Silver J. Movie Day at the Supreme Court on I Know When I See It. www.library.findlaw.com, May 2003.

Sipkoff M. Is pay for performance part of the cure or the problem? Managed Care, July 2005.

Smith M. What do patients expect? Therein lies the key to lawsuits. General Surgery News, November 2005.

Springer H. Back door into Fed court slammed shut. Medical Staff Leader, August 2006, pp. 1–2

Springer H. Pick up the phone. Medical Staff Leader, March 2004, pp. 1–4.

Sorrel A. Failure to diagnose is the no. 1 allegation in liability lawsuits. American Medical News, March 2006, p. 13.

Sorrel A. One computer theft spurs patient privacy lawsuit. American Medical News, March 2006, p. 7.

Sorrel A. Reservist sues after hospital calls in loan. American Medical News, March 2006, p. 11.

Steps to Prevent & Avoid Medical Errors. www.medicalmalpractice.com/prevention.

Sullivan M. Negotiate with patients on treatment of pain. American Medical News, April 2006, p. 13.

The Top Ten Medicaid Enrollment in Managed Care. AMNews.com, 2005.

Taylor M. JCAHO "unplugged": the band plays on. General Surgery News, February 2006, p. 24.

United-Pacificare merger troubles. Physicians AM News, 2005;48(28).

Weiss G. What About a Malpractice Surcharge. Medical Economics, 2004. www.memag.com.

Westlaw. California Legislative Service. Ch. 683 (A.B. 632), 2007.

What Are Medical Errors? www.medicalmalpractice.com/prevention-medical.

Winter E. Chasing medical dollars makes no sense. General Surgery News, February 2006, p. 20.

Your Health & The Law: How to Avoid Being a Victim of Malpractice. Physicians for Quality. www.pfq.com/malpractice.esp.

Zigmond J. Mediocre care prevalent: study. Modern Healthcare, March 2006, p. 12.

Index

Printed in the United States